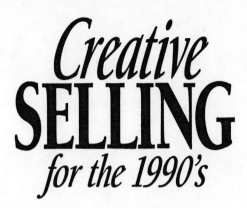

Creative
SELLING
for the 1990's

Ben Feldman

Creative SELLING
for the 1990's

Ben Feldman

Longman Financial Services Publishing
a division of Longman Financial Services Institute, Inc.

While a great deal of care has been taken to provide accurate and current information, the ideas, suggestions, general principles and conclusions presented in this book are subject to local, state and federal laws and regulations, court cases and any revisions of same. The reader is thus urged to consult legal counsel regarding any points of law—this publication should not be used as a substitute for competent legal advice.

Executive Editor: Kathleen A. Welton
Project Editor: Chris Christensen, Ellen Allen
Copy Editor: Gene DeRoin
Interior Design: Edwin Harris
Cover Design: Salvatore Concialdi

Published by Longman Financial Services Publishing
a division of Longman Financial Services Institute, Inc.

Printed in the United States of America.

89 90 91 10 9 8 7 6 5 4 3 2 1

Library of Congress Cataloging-in-Publication Data

Feldman, Ben, 1912–
   Creative selling / Ben Feldman.—3rd ed.
     p. cm.
   Previous ed. published under title: Creative selling for the seventies.
   Includes index.
   ISBN 0-88462-117-0
   1. Insurance—Agents. 2. Selling. 3. Insurance, Life—Agents.
I. Feldman, Ben, 1912–   Creative selling for the seventies.
II. Title.
HG8877.F44 1989
368.30292'00688—dc19   88-8408
                            CIP

This book is dedicated to Fritzie—my own beautiful brown-eyed Fritzie—for being with me—for listening to my problems—for always giving me something to hold on to—for helping me help others—and for always being there when I needed someone there ... I'm grateful. ...

—Ben

Foreword

Someone once remarked that if Ben Feldman didn't exist, he would have to have been "invented."

Many years ago as I left the Pittsburgh area for Home Office Assignment, I met Ben Feldman as he was beginning his extraordinary career! So it has been a special privilege to watch Ben's growth at close hand and see him achieve the reputation for being the man who "raised the sales sights of an industry."

Any man who has, single-handedly, put more than $1 billion on the life insurance books in one career has certainly earned the title of the country's most creative and hard-working agent. Who else then could be better qualified to write about creative salesmanship than Ben Feldman?

Today the million-dollar case has become rather routine in various home office underwriting departments—thanks to Ben's utterly contagious ability to think BIG! Today multi-million insurance proposals no longer raise eyebrows because Ben sought out big answers to big problems—because Ben thrives on multi-million-dollar challenges.

And throughout it all, Ben has remained humble and low key. And what does Ben worry about most? The big cases that get away! Not because of a lost commission, but because Ben knows that a big problem, unsolved, is still there. Somehow he feels the man with the big problem was "a better salesman than I was." Unsolved problems have always bothered Ben.

This book is typical of Ben's desire to share his philosophy and his methods with all who'll listen. How fortunate we are to be in the life insurance business at a time when we can take such tremendous inspiration from that gifted high school "drop-out" who has gone on to become a legend in his own time.

DUDLEY DOWELL
President, retired
New York Life Insurance Company

Contents

PART TWO

PART THREE

PART 1

Chapter 1

Don't Sell Life Insurance—Sell What Life Insurance Can Do

Can you give me an example of what you mean by that, Ben?

I had a case—an astute businessman. Know what he was worth? *Millions.* Know how much insurance he had? Practically none. Only $2,000. He became successful by making his dollars work real hard. And what is a hard-working dollar? A dollar that brings in a big return. That's why he was a millionaire—he didn't want to use his dollars in any *other* way. He did not want to put his dollars in insurance when they could be working much harder in his own business. He didn't want to stop growing, and he needed all the dollars he had.

But do you know something? As he grew, he needed more dollars. And one day he ran out of dollars. He had all those wonderful investment opportunities but he had no dollars to invest; all his dollars were tied up in other investments.

What did he do? What would you have done? He did exactly that: He went down to the bank to borrow some money. A *lot* of money. This man was a big investor. He needed big money. Is a million dollars big money? That's what this man did. He went to the bank and asked for a million dollars.

The banker said to him: "A million dollars? Well, that's a lot of money. Sure, we know you, and we know all about your success, and we know you'll make a lot of progress with that million dollars. But a million dollars! How long do you think it'll take you to pay it back?"

"Well," this man said, "I've worked out a projection." He showed the banker a sheet with a lot of figures on it. "Here are my investments, and here's what I can figure these investments will return me per year, and here's how long I can project it's going to take me to pay you back."

And how long was that? A good many years. It would be years and years before the bank would get its million dollars back.

The banker said to him: "How do we know you have that time? Suppose you run out of time—what happens to our money?"

The banker was right. If something happened to the man, what would happen to the bank's money? And something *could* happen. Tell me, do you know anyone who has a lease on life? No one has a lease on life. The banker wanted assurance that if this man died before he paid back the million dollars, the bank would still get back their money.

So the banker said to him: "How much insurance do you have?"

The man had to admit that he didn't have much insurance.

"What's it amount to?" the banker asked.

"Practically nothing."

"Practically nothing!" the banker said—not sounding at all like a friendly banker. "You mean to tell me you want us to put a value on your time of *one million dollars*, but the value *you yourself* put on your time is practically nothing! We just can't do it."

The banker turned him down. The banker would've been crazy to have done anything else.

Now, what did my man need in order to get that loan? Life insurance? Yes. But what did he really need—deep down? We're going back to basics; to fundamentals. What did he really need to get the money from the bank? What the man needed was *time*. Time to complete his plans. Time to pay back the million dollars. But he *couldn't guarantee* that he'd have the time—so what was he to do?

What the bank wanted was a guarantee that if the man ran out of time, on the day he walked out, a million dollars would walk in. And *when* could he run out of time? *Anytime.* Tomorrow. The next day. Does anyone know when time runs out? That million dollars had to be created *now*—ready to walk in *any-time*. And what can create a million dollars that fast? Life insurance. Nothing but life insurance.

So this man—who had refused to see me when I first began to call on him—said to me:

"Ben, I still don't need life insurance—but I sure can use what life insurance can do for me."

And what could life insurance *do* for him? He needed time to accumulate the money to pay back the loan. Life insurance guaranteed the money in case he ran out of time. *What did life insurance do for him? It underwrote time. Time to complete his plans. Time to do what had to be done.*

And isn't that the same with everyone? We all must die someday. Never at the right time. Always at the wrong time. We never have quite enough time to complete our plans, make our dreams come true—and that's why it's always the wrong time. Who'll give us more time? Only The Man Upstairs. But we can give our clients the equivalent of time—in the sense that we give them the money to complete their plans. You know, we sell contracts for time and money. We can't guarantee the time—but we *can* guarantee the money.

Chapter 2

The Basic Purpose of Life Insurance Is to Create Cash

Exactly how does life insurance buy time?

Pick up a policy. Read the front page again. What does it say? "We promise to pay." Pay *what*? "The face amount." When? "Immediately in case of death." Tell me, when will that be? It could be anytime. When that time comes, we walk in with—*what*? "The face amount." Cash that *guarantees* that a person can raise a family, continue a business, pay off a home, educate children, secure a spouse's welfare, complete every dream—*even though that person is no longer there!*

"The face amount." With a drop of ink, a piece of paper and a few pennies we create *instantly* what our prospect had hoped to accumulate *eventually*. How does life insurance buy time? By *creating* money. What else but life insurance can *create* money?

When someone buys an insurance policy, we put the face amount in escrow. That amount wasn't accumulated. It was created *for* the policyholder. You know, most people get their money by accumulating it—accumulating it slowly, painfully over the years. But our job is not to accumulate. Our job is to create. *What do we create? Dollars that underwrite time.*

The basic purpose of life insurance is to create cash: Nothing more, nothing less. Everything else just confuses the issue. Your job as a life insurance agent is to do what no one else can do. Do you know anyone else who can *create money?*

You know what I carry in my case? A thousand dollar bill. I'll walk up and open my case, and the prospect will look at the thousand dollar bill and say, "What's *that?*" And I'll say, pointing to the thousand dollar bill:

"That's what I sell. This thousand dollar bill comes in packages of a hundred. How many do you want?"

You can see the wonderful thing that you're selling: contracts for delivery of money.

Chapter 3

Life Insurance Creates Cash at a Discount When It's Needed Most

I've often heard you say you deliver "discounted dollars." What do you mean by that, Ben?

Sometimes I say to a prospect: "Give me two cents and I'll give you a dollar. I'll put that dollar in escrow. I'll write your name on it. I'll keep it in escrow for a year. If anything happens to you, we'll trade: I'll keep the two cents and you get the dollar. And at the end of the year, if nothing happens to you, I'll repeat the offer. One dollar for another year for two cents!"

And I'll repeat the offer year after year.

At two cents a year, it takes a long time to pay a dollar for a dollar, doesn't it? You know what kind of dollars you're buying? You're buying *discounted dollars*.

The two cents I talked about? That's the premium. For someone in their early fifties, the premium is about twenty dollars per thousand—and that's about two cents per dollar.

The premiums go up as you grow older. For a person in their fifties, I've got a dollar I'll sell for three cents. For someone in their sixties, I've got a dollar I'll sell for six cents.

Look at the life expectancy tables: The odds are a man will never pay in as much as we pay out. So the dollars we provide almost always come to a man at a discount. We don't only provide the dollars needed to complete a person's plans—we provide those dollars at a discount.

Do you see this wonderful thing the insurance industry has done? Look at this way: The insurance industry has designed a machine—a money-making machine—and it makes discounted dollars.

And when does it deliver those discounted dollars? *Exactly* when you need them; when time has run out, when there is no more time for you to complete your plans. Discounted dollars—to take the place of the time you no longer have. Discounted dollars—to make everything you want come true.

These discounted dollars are tax-free. I say to a prospect, "Here's an option on a dollar for one year at two cents. I guarantee the dollar. And when you pick up the option, your dollar is tax-free."

Go in and tell your prospect that what you're selling are contracts that *guarantee* the delivery of tax-free dollars at a discount. Insurance is the closest thing to getting something for nothing I've ever found.

Chapter 4

Sell Tailored Dollars

What do you mean when you say the discounted
dollars you sell are tailored?

Remember the businessman I talked about who needed
a loan from the bank? He wouldn't see me. He wouldn't
let me in the door until he had a *specific* problem.
What was it? A million dollars worth of credit. He didn't
want life insurance, but he did want what life insurance
would do for him—get him the credit he needed.

I'd say to this man: "Mr. Jones, you have a credit
problem. A million dollars. May I show you my idea?
The day you walk out, a million tax-free dollars walk
in. And you only pay a small fraction of that million
dollars." Tailored dollars to insure a credit line!

My work is to make the policies fit. You know,
when you buy a pair of pants or a pair of shoes, you

just can't buy any pair. You make sure they fit. Like a
tailor with a bolt of cloth, I make life insurance fit.
That's what I mean when I say I sell life insurance as
tailored dollars.

Can you give me another example of
tailored dollars—discounted dollars that help solve
a specific problem?

How about someone who leaves an estate? You
know, if the estate is any real size, Uncle Sam can take
a third of it. They call it taxes.

Say to this woman: "Mrs. Jones, you have a problem. No one has a lease on life and most people don't
die at the right time; there is no right time. Mrs. Jones,
the taxes must be paid *from* your estate—or *for* your
estate. Let me pay it *for* your estate—with discounted
dollars." Those are *tailored* dollars to pay estate taxes.

And there are so many, so many other specific
problems that tailored dollars can solve.

Chapter 5

Pinpoint the Problem

*Can you show me how you pinpoint
a prospect's problem?*

Tailored dollars help a person solve a specific problem. So one of the keys to selling is simply to look for the problem. If I find a problem that's going to cost you or your family money, you need insurance.

Make sure that you *have* found the problem, that you recognize it, that you understand it so well that you know the price of doing something about it, and the price of doing nothing about it. I will show you that by doing nothing, it will cost you dollars; but by doing something, it will cost you pennies.

So pinpoint the problem. Explain to the prospect that there's *a price tag* on doing something, and there's *a price tag* on doing nothing. The price tag on doing nothing is a lot higher in the end.

Here's an example of what I say to a prospect:

"You spent thirty years putting this company together. I've never known anybody who had a lease on life, do you? No? Then it's only a question of time until you walk out and Uncle Sam walks in. Know what he wants? Money! And he has a way of getting it. First. Not last. Could you, right now, give me thirty percent of everything you own—in cash? That's the least Uncle Sam will take. Could you give it to me without it hurting a little bit?

"You spend a lifetime locking money up in bricks and stone and steel. Someday, someone will have to unlock those bricks and convert them back into money. Wouldn't it be easier to let me do this for you? Then the day you walk out, $1 million walks in."

Chapter 6

The Problem Must Have a Price Tag

*Will you give me another demonstration of how you
sell by pinpointing a problem with a price tag?*

I might say something like this:

"You spend a lifetime making money, plowing it
back into a successful corporation, becoming quite
wealthy, worth a lot of money—and yet you have no
money. That is, money in the form of dollars. To keep
growing, you converted dollars into other assets. In
other words, you locked them up.

"But someday, you're going to have to *unlock* them.
And if you're not here, that may become a liquidation.
The other word for liquidation is quite often—*loss*.
You spend a lifetime accumulating assets; someone
will take them apart over night.

You're going to need some dollars, and I have dollars that are guaranteed and discounted. They cost pennies apiece. You never pay in the amount you are paid out. Furthermore, your gain is free of income tax. You're going to need money. Why can't you use my dollars? They cost pennies apiece!

"There's a price tag on everything. By doing nothing it will cost you dollars. By doing something it will cost you pennies."

Chapter 7

Create Specific Ideas for Specific Problems

First, you start with a *problem*. The problem must have a price tag. Then you create *specific ideas* for *specific problems*. You know, ideas are the keys that unlock a case. Once your prospect has accepted the idea, he's bought the insurance. Show your prospects simple, easy-to-understand ideas that tell them how they can solve their problems.

You're not selling insurance. You're selling ideas— ideas to solve a person's problems.

Ben, I assume that you have come up with many ideas for solving specific problems. Will I be able to use them when I sell?

There are so many good ideas—some mine, some from others—none completely original. You're welcome to use my ideas. If you work with them, they'll become your ideas.

If you can get just one idea that will work for you, one idea that can start you thinking bigger, then this book will have been worthwhile and you'll be on your way.

Perhaps an idea can start you thinking bigger and can raise your sights. You know, you're only as big as you think you are. There's no limit to what you can do.

Chapter 8

Package
Your Ideas

What do you mean when you say you "package" your ideas to solve a person's problem?

The key to a sale is the idea, and the key to selling the idea is to package it.

When I was just beginning to sell, I would say: "You want to be sure your daughter goes to college? May I show you this idea ...?" And what was the idea? It was an *education package*. It wasn't insurance this man wanted; he wanted his daughter to go to college. So I didn't talk about anything else. I showed him how we could guarantee that his daughter would go to college—and I used words and figures he was sure to understand. That was my package.

Or I would say to a businesswoman, "How would you like to retire with a guaranteed income for the rest of your life? Here's an idea I have. May I show it to you?" What she wanted was a guaranteed retirement income—not insurance. And I showed her how to get what she wanted. That's *all* I showed her. I made it very direct, very easy to understand. And that was my retirement *package*.

I had lots of packages for different purposes. I would say to a prospect, "I have a special package of money designed for people like you." Each package was different. I'd have each package worked out in my own head so I could talk about it clearly and a prospect could understand what I was talking about. I sold simple packages designed to help people with their problems.

Chapter 9

Keep Your Packages Simple

When you started out, your packages were simple. Do you mean to say that now, when you sell big-dollar packages, you can still keep your packages simple?

The key to packaging an idea is to make it simple. Insurance tends to be complex. I can't understand it unless it's simple. The simpler the better. When something is simple, it's easier to sell than when something is complicated. To sell something, make it easy to understand—and you do that when you keep it simple.

You know something? I don't do anything different these days. I still sell packages. Do you know what I call myself? A package salesman. I create and sell simple clean-cut packages, each with a purpose, a single-minded purpose. The purpose is to solve a problem that's very serious—very real, very real. So a person *needs* and *must have* my package.

Ben, how did you get the idea of selling life insurance in the form of simple packages?

One of the things I learned early was that you have to know what you're doing. So I would spend hour after hour with the rate book until I knew it inside out, upside down. There were all kinds of contracts in it, and I learned them. You see, the rate book, basically, is just mechanics—2 plus 2 makes 4. I had to make sure a policy didn't make 5; that it only made 4. I had to understand it, and I couldn't understand it unless I made it simple. So it became simple.

Then I could fit the prospect like a tailor would fit a suit from a bolt of cloth. I could create a simple package to solve a problem. I would give my packages names. They were nothing but blocks of whole life, but I'd call them: Special policy designed to educate your little boy; special spouse policy; For partners: a see-saw policy; if one gets off, the other falls off.

After making up one special little package, I'd make up a list of names and I'd begin making my calls. "Let me show you a package of money designed for you." I was making some sales—and the sun was shining. But after a while, you know what would happen? The package would get old. It was still good, but I would lose my enthusiasm. You know what I would do then? I would make up another little package, and I'd give it a new name. And I would make up another list, and I'd go out again calling.

Ben, you said your packages were really blocks of whole life. Are they still blocks of whole life? What I mean is: today, life insurance companies are marketing many different products—mutual funds, for example. Exactly what kind of life insurance product do you package, Ben?

You hear a lot about various types of products that are marketed by life insurance companies. What are they? Mutual funds, variable life, many things designed to go the way the economy goes—up or down or both. Well, you know if a person wants to make a lot of money, he or she must take a lot of risks. Tell me, what happened to the stock market in the last couple of years? It was up. Fine. Then it went down. Not so fine. That's not the kind of foundation I want for myself and my family or for the people depending on me. I'd like to be sure that when I'm gone there's something there—a real foundation—something my people can depend on.

You know, many of us spend a lifetime putting things together and then see all we built up falling apart. Our plans for the family, our business, the people we worked with—all falling apart. All our dreams—dreams that we built up slowly over the years, brick by brick—all our dreams ending in a crash. So I think we must build something strong, solid, firm—guaranteed. We must ask, "Will what I'm building on keep all I've built up from falling apart?"

We must know that there will always be something there that's absolutely dependable, so that when our family needs it, they'll have it. I think you'll find when the chips are down, a person will buy life insurance for its certainty—for the assurance that what was built up won't fall apart.

Sometimes I say, "Your life insurance is so basic to the security of your family. The day you fall apart, all you have could fall apart. Creditors come first, your family comes second. But not if you build a personal program that provides basic security to your family.

You know, the policy helps you protect your family against creditors in many ways. In the state of Ohio there's even a 'spendthrift clause' in the policy. Know what it does? It makes the proceeds of the policy free from creditors' claims, so even if you were a spend-thrift, your family would still be secure. Your family has the right to go on living—and life insurance pro-tects that right. Let me show you how. . . ."

There's no substitute for life insurance. There never was and there never will be. There's no investment you could make that's anything like it. Why? What's the best investment? The one that pays the most when it's needed most. And, tell me, isn't that life insurance?

So what I sell is whole life. That's to secure the future. And I sell term. That's an option on the future. And I put these policies into packages.

Chapter 10

Sell Big Packages

*What's the difference between the packages you sell
now and the packages you sold when you first
started out?*

The packages are bigger now. All problems have price
tags—some are simply bigger than others. My cases
are bigger these days simply because the problems I
solve have bigger price tags. When you create a package, make it big enough to do the job. Don't underestimate your prospect's needs.

Why did you start out with small packages?

I hadn't learned how to think big. Do you know
how I started out selling insurance?

I lived in a little town, population about 1,500
people. The town was Salineville, Ohio, where my

father set up a family business. My parents bought and sold produce, cattle, hogs, chickens, eggs, and it was a case of everybody pitching in and doing his part. We were by no means well-to-do. Our family was large, nine children, and my parents felt it important for me to chip in and carry my load. Dad paid me $5 per week. That was enough. I was living at home, and I didn't need any more money.

The years went by and some of the young kids were driving cars. I didn't have one. I sure wanted one, and I finally persuaded my Dad to give me a raise. He raised me to $10 a week, and the first thing I did was to go out and buy a new car. A Model-T Ford. I remember I was paying $25 a month for it. Since I was earning only $40 a month, it sure didn't give me much leeway to drive the car, but I did—and I finally got the car paid for. Well, you know what goes with a car?

Girls!

I knew one of the most gorgeous girls in the world. I began calling. And slowly, surely, time went by, and we wanted to get married. One day she really jarred me. She said that I couldn't support her on $10 a week. So, it seemed to me that I wasn't really needed at home, and I had better get myself a better paying job. Where do you look for a job in a little town of 1,500 people?

A friend of mine was working for an insurance company, and there just happened to be an opening. I knew he was earning $35 a week, which to me was a fabulous amount of money. I went down and applied for the job. The roof fell in. I didn't seem to measure up in any way, shape, or form. I was shy, I was backward, I talked with a lisp. I hadn't even finished high school. They tossed me out.

But a positive mental attitude, *that* more than anything else determines your success. If you decide you are going to feel wonderful, strong, excited—then you have the power to move mountains. I had this attitude. I never take "no" for an answer. If they throw me out one door, I'll come in another. So I came back, and I came back. And I finally got the job!

My friend was making $35 a week, but not me! I remember the very first week on the job, I wrecked my car. And when Saturday rolled around, I found I had earned $15 and couldn't get my car out of hock because the bill was more than $15.

I worked with this company on the debit. On a debit you're responsible primarily for collection, and I didn't like to collect. I wanted to call on people, to try to make sales. I would give the collection book to my assistant manager. He'd make my collections. I'd go calling. We'd meet at the end of the day, and by then I'd have some sales. My debit would grow. It got so big that one man couldn't handle it. So each year the company would cut it in half and put another man on. This went on for three years until I got a chance to go with New York Life.

It was a big step. I wasn't quite sure I wanted to do it, and finally I did it on a trial basis. I was told, "Come on in and try it for 90 days, and if you don't like it, you can leave."

Meanwhile, I got an opinion from the debit company: "O.K. try it, but it won't work out. It just can't. At the end of 90 days come back."

I still wasn't sure I wanted to change jobs. Then the debit company said to me, "You'll never make good. You'll fall flat on your face. You shouldn't go at all. It's not for you."

And that did it! I decided I *would* make the change and I would *never* go back no matter what happened.

To answer your question, "Why did I start out with small packages?" Even when I got to New York Life, I was thinking debit size. I was thinking small.

Who helped you start thinking big?

When I started with New York Life, somehow I got the impression that it was normal to write ten cases a week. So I would report in on Friday afternoon, and I usually had my ten cases. Oh, they weren't big. I was still thinking debit size.

At one of my very first meetings, Isaac Kibrick, that great salesman, was the guest of honor. In that particular month I had written 40 cases, and I was so flattered when he singled me out for praise. My cases were small, but, he said, "Your cases will grow. Some will become $10,000 cases and some $25,000. Some, maybe, $50,000. And some, maybe, even more."

The cases *did* grow. Why? The people grew, and I was tagging along; and as they grew, I grew.

There are so many, many men and women to whom I am indebted, and yet if I were to try and single out one, it would be Andy Thomson, formerly of our home office, because he, more than anyone else, gave me a track to run on. The track had to be simple or I couldn't stay on it. The track was three cases a week—just three cases a week.

"Pay no attention to the size of the case," Andy said. "The size of the case will grow as the years go by, as the people grow. You will grow in your thinking, your knowledge, your know-how."

You know, that's exactly what happened. Let me tell you about my first sale, as an example.

He was a boyhood friend of mine—from the same town. He wanted to buy a policy. I didn't know quite what he wanted or how to put it together. He wasn't quite sure of what he wanted either. He just wanted to buy the first policy that I'd write. So we both went down to the office manager, and we put together a $5,000, 20-pay Life. I was really walking on the clouds!

As the years went by, this little case grew. I could see that each day this man was trading the day for the dollar, and he wrapped the dollar back into a growing, expanding company. As his problems became bigger, his program became bigger. I had learned to "tag along behind your people, and as they grow, you'll grow." That's what happened in this little case. It grew and it grew and it grew. When I came to sell my first million-dollar policy, you know who I sold it to? *That* man, my first sale!

Remember, as time goes by, people grow—and as they grow, quite often their problems grow. The need is greater. So the solution must be greater.

What do you do different now when you sell big policies from when you sold small ones?

I'm not doing anything different now from 20 years ago. If my package is big, it's because the prospect's problem has a big price tag. And you know something? —someday that price must be paid. It's true, the prospect doesn't *have* to pay it. But if *he* doesn't pay it—and remember, we're talking about big price tags, price tags worth hundreds of thousands of dollars, sometimes millions—if *he* doesn't pay it, *his family* will *have* to pay it. And they'll have to pay it with *hundred-cent dollars*. Isn't it better for *him* to pay it since he can do so with *discounted dollars?*

Whether a prospect buys my package or not, there's a price tag either way—and *somebody* has to pay. Isn't it better for the family breadwinner to pay *pennies* instead of the family paying dollars? So even though the price tag is big, the policyholder pays very little for it. A person may need half a million dollars, but will pay very little for that money.

And when you show your prospect all that, when you show him or her the price tag is very real—when you show that it must be paid—and when you show that you can pay it *for* him or her *no matter how big it is*—and the cost will be pennies not dollars—then your prospect will see the *need* for what you're presenting. You'll be on your way to a sale. A *big* sale.

Chapter 11

To Sell Larger Policies—Build Up Your Own Program

I confess I get a little tongue-tied when it comes to talking about big money. What can I do?

Years ago when I got started, I wrote $500 policies, and the reason they weren't smaller was that there wasn't anything smaller. And you know what was wrong? I didn't have much insurance. I think I had two thousand dollars worth. And most everyone I spoke to had *that*—or more. I was afraid of my prospects. Why? Because they were bigger than I was; I was looking up at them. It's much harder to make a sale when you're looking up. It's very hard, very hard to make a sale when the prospect looks like a giant. He or she has ten thousand dollars worth of insurance and I've got two thousand, and I'm telling my *prospect* to buy more. You know who should buy more? *I* should buy more.

So I began buying insurance for myself. I was starting out in life; I didn't have the money. At that time, I was buying insurance for which it seemed I couldn't pay. It's a funny thing: I had no money, but I *found* the money. And you know, you start out like that and then a wonderful thing happens! *If you buy more, you sell more.* It's your clients who pay the premiums for your policies. *Do it*—you'll find it *will* work for you.

So I built up my program. And then I finally built myself up to where I had $50,000 worth of insurance. What happened? I found myself talking to a person with $100,000 worth of insurance. I had just $50,000! I was ashamed to have so little. In those days, if I were talking to a person who had $100,000 and I had $50,000, I would look up to that person. He or she was bigger than I was, and I was scared.

So what did I do? I pulled myself up. But when I had $200,000, know what happened? There I was talking to somebody with $300,000. I was still afraid. So I continued increasing my personal program.

And you know, when you do, you feel *big*. When you have $500,000 and the person you're talking to has *only* $300,000—oh boy! You enjoy talking to that person.

The fact is, when you raise your sights, you raise the other person's sights. And when you raise his sights, you're helping him because his problem has a big price tag, and only *you* can pay it for him. Isn't that a good thing?

So build your *own* insurance program. The best way to sell something is to first own it yourself. I'm not frightened to propose a million–dollar policy to any person.

As a rule, *you will sell each year ten times the amount of insurance you own.* Build your own program up to one million dollars, and you'll be writing ten million dollars a year.

Your prospects grow, and if you stay with them, you'll grow with them. Continue to study. Continue to build your own program.

Chapter 12

How to Write Twelve Million Dollars in the Next Six Months

Don't be afraid to dream big dreams. They have a way of coming true. Strange as it seems, your biggest problem is to sell yourself. Most people exchange their lifetime for much too little. Don't be afraid to think big. Anything your mind can conceive, *that* you can achieve. Think small, and your cases will be small. Think big, and your cases will be big.

If you want big volume, you have to look for prospects with big price tags on their problems. How would you like to write twelve million dollars in the next six months? Of course you would. But you can't do it without big packages.

*Even with big packages, Ben, twelve million dollars—
that's an awful lot of money. You must have some
secret—some special way of doing it. Have you?*

What you're saying is: Twelve million dollars! I'd
have to run so fast in six months, it doesn't look like
it's possible. It's too big. I don't think I can do it.

But listen, and I'll tell you how to do it.

Take $12 million and break it apart into months:
divide by six, and what have you got? Two million
dollars a month. Still too big? All right, break it down
some more. How many weeks are there in a month?
Four. Divide $2 million by four. Now what have you
got? $500,000 a week. Now continue to break it down:
Break down that $500,000 into three cases a week. Now
you have less than $200,000 a case. All you need is to
write two or three cases totaling $500,000 each week.
If you miss today, know what? You'll make it tomorrow.

Now it's do-able. You *can* do it. You can achieve
your goal. But you've got to start off with a goal—a big
goal. Why a big goal? You have to have a goal in the
back of your mind—let's call it a dream—big enough
to be *exciting*. Because unless it's exciting, it won't
make you run. Twelve million dollars in the next six
months! *That's* exciting. That's something big enough
to get excited about. If it's not big enough to get excited about, you won't do it. So set a goal big enough
to get excited about. Then make the goal do-able.

Start with a goal—a big goal that makes you excited. Then break it down into three cases a week.
That's your deadline. You've got to run so far, so fast.
Now you've got a track to run on. The key to the goal
is the deadline. You must have goals and deadlines.
One isn't good without the other. But together they
can be tremendous.

I started off years ago with a goal of three cases a week. When my cases got bigger, my volume got bigger.

Ben, what's the average size of your case?

I think this year so far I have $48 million on 20 cases. That averages out to about $2.4 million a case.

Chapter 13

To Find the Big Case, Find the Person with a Big Problem

It's clear to me that if you're going to sell a case in seven figures, you've got to find a prospect with a seven-figure problem that life insurance can solve. What kind of problem is that?

What you're really saying is, "Why are some cases bigger than others?"

The only difference is between little problems and big problems. And where do you find the biggest problems? In estate tax situations, in close corporations, in partnerships. There are many packages to solve these kinds of problems.

How do you find a prospect with these kinds of problems?

I'm driving down the road, and see a sign over the door of a building: *The ABC Manufacturing Company.* It looks like a pretty sizable operation.

Now the next thing I do is get a D&B report. That's a financial report on the ABC Company, which comes to you from Dun and Bradsteet, D&B. You can subscribe to their service. You can get a report, a D&B, on any company from them.

I've got the D&B—what do I do with it? I study it. I go over it very carefully. Now I know who owns the ABC Company. I find out it's a closely held corporation. The person who runs it is the person who owns it.

Now the next thing I look at is: What is owned? What is owed? Is there a lot of money or a lot of debts?

Say I find out there isn't that much loose money floating around. This is a million-dollar business, but that million dollars is locked up in brick and steel and land and machinery. All the money is in the business, not in cash.

What else do I know after reading this report?

Tell me, wouldn't it be logical to assume that the owner has a house, owns a car, and has piled up certain investments, certain expensive possessions. So here's someone with an estate of maybe seven, eight hundred thousand dollars.

Then I know this: Uncle Sam wants two hundred thousand, three hundred thousand dollars from this owner that's the part of the estate that *isn't* the owner's. So this person has a problem—a big problem—a problem with a big price tag.

"I have a package of money that will pay your estate taxes. With discounted dollars. Let me show it to you. . . ."

Ben, I'd like to get back to the way you said you get started when you prospect for a big case. You said: you're driving down the road and you see a sign that says ABC Company, and if it looks like a sizable company, you look into it. Is that what you'd advise me to do?

Well, I do it, and it seems to work. But I'll tell you what you can do also. You can use a Directory—a Business Directory of your area, if there is one. You can go down the list and pick some companies that look large enough and get their D&Bs and get started that way.

You know, I also get leads from reading the papers and from referrals. Sometimes I know people who know a prospect. So I ask questions, discreet questions. I compile as much information on the prospect as I can.

When you're studying your D&B and sifting through all the other facts, look for problems in those three big-price-tag areas—estates, close corporations, partnerships. And that's how you find the prospect with the big-price-tag problems.

Chapter 14

Get Out of
the Office

*When you've lined up your suspects, how do you make
contact with them? Many agents I know put their
feet up on a desk and pick up the phone.*

That's so wrong, so wrong. You're not selling when
you're sitting in your office.

You know what I do sometimes after I've checked
out my leads and suspect they have problems?

I make up a list of these suspects. Some of them I
know *have* problems. So they're not suspects; they're
prospects. I make up a list, and I take a month—not to
make sales, but just to call on people. I'm going out to
find people. But special people. People with problems. I'm taking time to say hello to people with
problems.

Do you just go in cold?

I have, and I've seen many cold calls turn into sales. But what I do now is this: To that list of suspects and prospects I've worked up, I send this out on a monthly basis:

Personal

Appointment

Record

of

for

April

1988

APRIL

It's very useful in helping a person keep appointments. Even the back is useful because there's a scratch pad on it, and there's a place to mark down future appointments.

APRIL 1988

SUNDAY	MONDAY	TUESDAY	WEDNESDAY	THURSDAY	FRIDAY	SATURDAY
					1	2
3	4	5	6	7	8	9
10	11	12	13	14	15	16
17	18	19	20	21	22	23
24	25	26	27	28	29	30

BEN FELDMAN, C.L.U.
NEW YORK LIFE INSURANCE CO.
MEMBER OF MILLION DOLLAR ROUND TABLE

Premier Bldg., P.O. Box 30
East Liverpool, Ohio 43920
Phone (216) 385-4600

The person I call on gets these "Personal Appointment Records" month after month. He or she uses them and gets to know my name. I also send out letters from time to time—and there are a number of them in the book Andy Thomson wrote about me.*

So when I walk in and say to a secretary, "I'm Ben Feldman and I'd like to get acquainted with Mr. Jones," and the secretary picks up the intercom and says, "Mr. Jones, Mr. Feldman is here to see you," he'll know who Ben Feldman is. Maybe—because he knows who I am and wants to say thanks for the "Personal Appointment Records," or because one or two of my letters caught his attention—he'll ask me to come in.

---

*The Feldman Method, Andrew H. Thomson, Longman Financial Services Publishing, Chicago, IL.

Chapter 15

Make the Calls and the Sales Will Follow

Ben, I'm sure that not everyone agrees to see you when you walk in. What do you do then?

You're right, maybe a person won't see me. Maybe a secretary will tell me he's too busy. And chances are he *is* too busy. Everyone has priorities, first things first—and does he know that I'm there to solve a problem for him? He doesn't. So why should I be first priority. Not yet, I'm not first priority. But I will be. I know I will be. So I say goodbye, and I plan to come back. And I *do* come back.

Or sometimes a person will come out to see you just to tell you that they can't see you. Why do they come out? Because they're business people—they're selling something, too, in their own way, no matter what their position in the company, and they want people to be courteous to them when they're selling. Most people are courteous. When they don't want to see you, they won't have their secretaries brush you off. They'll come out and meet you, maybe in the hallway. So say to this kind of person, "I just want to meet you. I have some ideas that may be of interest to you. I'd like to come back." What can he say—*don't* come back? Or you can say, "I represent New York Life. I've heard a lot about you. I'd like to say hello and show you some ideas that could help you with your business. I'd like to come back." Maybe that's as far as you'll get the first time. But you'll *come back.* You'll *come back.*

Don't take no for an answer. Keep coming back. Sooner or later if the person is in the right mood and has a few minutes to spare, he'll say, "O.K., come on in. Glad to see you, but we'll have to make this fast." You have to work fast, make an impression fast. So say to this person, "May I show you something?" And this may be a probate record, showing how the day *before* some famous person died that person owed almost nothing, but the day *after* he died, that person's estate owed Uncle Sam hundreds of thousands or millions of dollars. This captures your prospect's attention, so you can continue: "Look what happens to very successful people. You know what your problem is? You've been too successful. This can happen to you. Now, I have some ideas that may be of interest. I'd like to come back."

Come back. That's so important, so important. *Come back.* Have you heard the story of the agent who kept coming back, and coming back, and coming back? When they closed one door in his face, he came in another door? And this kept on and on and on. So finally, the prospect—he was a good guy, he didn't want to be rude—finally, the prospect had to say,

"Please. I appreciate your enthusiasm. But, please don't come back for at least another five years." And the agent says, "O.K., I'll come back in five years. But if you're not here, who shall I ask for?"

That's what you have to do—just keep coming back.

How many calls on the average do you have to make before the call develops into an interview?

Sometimes, I have to make many, many calls.

But, you know, a call is a funny thing. Sometimes, when a person sees you, just a few words that you say can develop into an interview there and then. That's why you must make the calls. There's no substitute for making calls. Make the calls and sales will follow.

Ben, I understand that you make as many as 40 calls a month. You're very successful, and I know you have a big office. How do you manage it?

Yes, I have a busy office, a very busy office, and there are lots of things to be done, and they are done, but I still have time to go around and find prospects. You know why? I'll give you one reason:

I try not to go flying all over the map. I try to stay in my neck of the woods. My home is in East Liverpool, Ohio. I normally work within an area of 40 to 50 miles from it. Traveling, for the most part, is wasting time because there are many, many people in my own backyard. I can call on them and still have time to do all the things that have to be done. In spite of the fact that I do consider traveling to be wasting time, I find myself working in other cities. I work in New York. I work in Pittsburgh. I work in Florida. We have homes in Pittsburgh and Florida, and while I am there, I am constantly prospecting and trying to find new clients.

Chapter 16

Prospecting: People Plus Ideas

Do you always uncover a prospect's problem before you make a call?

Not always.

Then what do you do?

I go in and try to discover the problem face to face.

How do you do that?

I prospect basically with ideas—ideas to merchandise clean-cut, simple packages.

"Mr. Jones, I have money for sale. At a discount. You'll need that money some day to pay your taxes. May I present an idea that has been very valuable to a lot of people?"

Or:

Mrs. Smith, I have an idea that I think will be of interest. Are you interested in some tax-free money? You may need it some day to keep your company alive. I can help you develop that money. Will you listen?"

When prospecting, approach the person with a problem with disturbing questions. Keep asking disturbing questions, and sooner or later you'll find the specific problem. When you talk to a prospect, you know what's important? Listening. Learn to listen. That is how you will find the problem.

Prospecting is basically recognizing the problem and making sure the problem has a price tag. And you know something? When you find a prospect by pinpointing the problem, nine times out of ten, that prospect will become a policyholder.

Chapter 17

The Best Prospect

How would you define the best prospect, Ben?

The best prospect is a man or woman with a problem—all kinds of assets, but no money.

Where do you find the best prospects?

Among my clients. Why? Because my clients are prospects for *another* policy—for bigger coverage. Do you know that the biggest sales I have made to close corporations—and I've worked with hundreds of them—were made to corporations where I had *already made sales.*

A lot of us write policies, then run away. Then somebody else comes along and writes another policy for the client we ran away from—and that new policy turns out to be *a bigger one than the policy we had placed*. So continue to prospect among your clients.

I'm sure that not all my clients are prospects for more insurance. How can I tell which of my clients are prospects?

Watch them—and see which ones grow. The ones that grow—they're your prospects. You know, your people will grow—some of them, maybe all of them. And if you stay with them, *you'll* grow with them. I told you, my first sale was to a young businessman. A $2,000 policy. But he grew and I stayed with him, and, later on, he became the first man to buy a million dollar policy from me.

Why do I continue to sell to close corporations that I've already sold? Because they're growing—bringing in new key people—needing more working capital—getting bigger problems every day. I stay with them. When they have bigger problems, I call on them. My job—you know what it is? It's to solve those problems.

You know, cases will grow. There's no ceiling. Just stay with them, and you'll grow, too.

Chapter 18

Looking Down the Road

I've heard that you can't always wait until a client has grown to sell him insurance. You look into your clients' future and find their problems. Then you sell them today the insurance they'll need tomorrow. Is that right?

Yes. I call that looking down the road. I say to a prospect:

"You need $1 million to pay the taxes *today*—and here's a policy to cover it. But I know your company's making money, I know you're in good health, so I have another policy—and this is for *tomorrow. I'm looking down the road ten years.* Then, you'll need $2 million to pay your tax.

"And another thing: Your spouse has a right to income. So I have one designed for your salary continuation. It pays your spouse $100,000 a year for ten years. When you walk out, your income goes on. Don't you want that for your mate?"

Ben, most of us base the amount of insurance a person should have on current income. That's the accepted way. Do you think the accepted way of fixing the amount of life insurance a person should leave is wrong?

I do. Another man's life isn't worth the same as mine just because we have the same income *now*. Now—is that forever? Doesn't a person *grow*? Some don't grow, of course. But some *do*. Some of my clients have grown from local businesspeople to heads of national corporations. So what do I try to do when I see them growing? And you can see when a company is growing, the signs are clear to read. What do I do? I try to look down the road, see their problems that don't yet exist but will exist someday.

I can see that future problems can mean today's sales. But how can I convince a prospect to buy today for something not needed until tomorrow?

You're doing your client a great service when you pinpoint the problems ahead and show him or her how *tomorrow's needs go up*, but if one waits until tomorrow, *rates go up*—and *chances of getting life insurance go down*. So, tell me, isn't it better to buy now?

If a man can't afford whole life—and if he's growing, he may not be able to afford whole life—sell him term. You know what term is? It's an option on the future. He'll buy term *now*.

So—*sell ahead* and continue to look down the road among those clients you already *have* sold ahead to. One of my clients now has over $50,000,000 worth of insurance with me. He's still growing, and I don't think he'll ever stop. I look down the road, and I'm sure he needs $50 million more. What for? He has dreams, and he needs all that $100 million to build a foundation under his dreams. I can help him make his dreams come true.

Chapter 19

The Phone: Say What You Have to Say, Then Get Off

Ben, how do you set up the appointment for the interview once you've made a call and you're coming back? I know you often don't use the phone when you make your first calls, but don't you use the phone to set up an appointment when you're coming back or when you want to see an old client?

Of course I use the phone. But let me tell you something about telephones. Before you pick up the telephone, plan the words you're going to use. Know exactly what you're going to say. Say it. Then get off.

Sometimes, you know, I set up my first call by phone. This is my telephone approach:

"I represent New York Life. I've heard about you and would like to meet you. I specialize in discounted dollars. May I show you what I mean?"

Or suppose the man is a client and I know he's growing, and I know his problem will be growing in the future. I get on the phone and say:

"Mr. Jones, you know something? You're a successful man. Most successful men are running so hard they never look far enough down the road. May I show you what I mean?"

Or, sometimes when I phone to set up an interview date after I've already made a call, I put the woman's problem in the form of a question.

"Ms. Jones, how would you like to buy your partner's interest for pennies on the dollar? May I show you what I mean?"

"Sure, Ben, I'd like you to show me."

Then I say, "Would Tuesday at three or Friday at two be better?"

I give her a choice: one or the other. Not just one—not just, "How about Tuesday at three?" because she might say, "Sorry, Ben, I'm tied up then." I give her a choice, and she's got to make a decision: one or the other.

"O.K., Ben, I'll look forward to seeing you Friday at two."

That's all you do on the phone. You can't sell successfully on the phone. Don't waste your ammunition.

Chapter 20

How to Get a Prospect's Attention

Ben, I have this problem when I go in on an inter-
view: I talk to a prospect but he doesn't listen. His
mind is on other things. What should I do?

You know, there are a hundred ways to close a case,
but there has to be a beginning. And the beginning is
getting the prospect's attention.

I walk in and I flip open my case, and the prospect
looks at what I've got in it and says, "What's *that?*"

And I say, "It's what I sell. These come in packages of one hundred. How many packages would you
like?" And you know what I sell? A thousand dollar
bill! That gets the prospect's attention.

What does the prospect see? *A thousand dollar*
bill and two shiny new pennies.

Now, why should I carry a thousand dollar bill?
It's money. And money's funny—people like to look

at money. And two pennies—that makes them won-der. "Why the two pennies, Ben? What do they mean?"

I reply: "I'm selling dollars. For two pennies each."

Now the prospect's going to *listen*. Money usually does this, especially when it appears that the money is pretty much something for nothing.

The money—it might look like it's something for nothing, but prospects know it can't be. "What's it all about, Ben?" They want to know more.

When you get a person's attention, you know what you've done? You've done one of the most important things of all. It's the key. Why? The start of a sale is the interview. But the start of the interview is getting their attention. Unless you get their attention, you'll go no place.

Chapter 21

The Key to the Interview Is the Disturbing Question

Can you tell me what the purpose of the interview is as you see it, Ben?

The interview is to explore, to disturb, to pinpoint the problem, to move ahead by implied consent to the point when I say, "Let me put it together. You need a medical examination." I arrange it, and we go from there.

What, in your estimation, determines the success of an interview?

The key to the sale is the interview, and the key to the interview is the disturbing question. I say to a prospect, "How much is time worth to you?" Or, "Could you give me one-third of everything you own *right now* without it hurting a little bit?" Or, "Would you like to insure one year's profits?"

In the interview, logic isn't enough. Use logic and emotion. Get the prospect stirred up. There's nothing like a disturbing question to build a fire under a person.

Chapter 22

How to Close an Interview: "Let Me Put It Together . . ."

You said that you end the interview by saying "Let me put it together . . ." That means you don't try for a sale at the interview, do you?

That's correct. I say, "Let me put it together and you take a look."

"All right," the prospect will say, "you work it out and bring it back."

What's he or she got to lose? And even if he says nothing, he doesn't say "no." So you can still work it out and bring it back. In either case, what you've done is lead the prospect to give you *implied* consent.

How can he say, "No"? You're not forcing him to make a decision. You're not backing him into a sale. Never back a man into a corner and make him make a decision. Don't push. Lead.

Chapter 23

Get Them Examined and They're Three-Quarters Sold

What if the prospect says, "An examination! Not again! I've just had one and my doctor tells me I'm in wonderful shape." What do I do, Ben?

You know what you ought to say to that prospect? "Yes, you're in wonderful shape now. But your doctor didn't tell you how you'll be *ten years from now*. You see, we're going to take a look at how long you're going to live. Don't you want to know?"

He wants to know.

Say to him, "Suppose I set it up?"

What if he says, "Oh, I can't spare the time for a medical exam"? What do I say?

Say to this prospect, "You know, we may be pin-pointing your problem, but we may find there's very little we can do about it. Medically, I mean. Let's find out."

And you know something? Now that he's implied that he wants insurance, it worries him that he may not be able to get it. If you see him hesitating, disturb him more. Say: "I'm not sure at this point if all this talk about solving your problem is not a little premature. You know, there's a price tag on success. You know what that price tag is? A man gradually begins to fall apart. His pressure goes up. This goes wrong, that goes wrong. And, you know, you wait too long. The medical committee—well, the price you pay for success is certainly not going to help you with them. But, anyway, let's see. Let's see how much our life underwriting committee feels your life is worth."

I sometimes get a prospect who says, "There's nothing wrong with me." How do I get her to get an exam?

Say to this woman: "Let me make sure you're as good on the inside as you look on the outside. Could be you've waited too long. As the years go by, a person pays a price for success. Mother nature makes us a little bit older. And older doesn't mean better. Let's see if you can qualify."

Now, just because she thinks she may not be able to get it, she wants it. Now she *wants* to qualify. She'll *take* the exam.

Just how successful are you, Ben, in getting a person to take an examination?

When I say to a prospect, "Let's find out if I can get this for you. All I need now is underwriting, which means a medical examination. Suppose I set it up. Then I'll put it together, and you can take a look at what I have." Nine times out of ten, they'll go along. I haven't forced anyone into a decision. I won't let them make a decision. I'll wait for the medical O.K. No sense selling the policy until I can get it. Don't sell the policy first. Get it first.

Chapter 24

The Sale:
Getting Ready
to Get Ready

*Suppose I get a medical O.K. How do I
present the policy?*

Thoroughly understand the policy that you're going to
propose and why you picked the policy and why you
picked the amount. Thoroughly understand the plan
and what it will do for the applicant. Let there be no
doubt in your mind that you understand why he needs
the policy and why he needs that much coverage. Let
me say to you that the more you know about the
applicant and his family and what he wants done and
why he wants it done, the better able you are to fit the
policy to the man. I've told you already, selling insurance is like a tailor with a bolt of cloth. It'll be up to
you to make it fit.

How do I make a policy fit a prospect?

Is one prospect like another? Are one person's problems like another person's problems? Everyone is different. Everyone's problems are different. When you begin to work out the details, you see the differences. Two estate packages—they're different. The details are different. You've got to work out these details. That's the way you fit a policy to a prospect. I spend more time creating the case in my mind than I do selling it. I work it over and over again. Just when I get to the point where I *believe* it—where I'm sure it's right for the prospect—suddenly, I'm not so sure—suddenly, I want to make a change. And I do just that. I change it. So my office staff—they think I'm crazy. But I must know I'm right and that the policy is right for the prospect. I call all this getting ready to get ready.

How much time should I spend getting ready
to get ready?

Be careful about overdoing things—taking too much time. So many people spend so much time getting ready that they never get ready. Take just enough time to get the job done right. When a job is right, you know it—because you believe it. Any more time than enough time is wasted time.

Chapter 25

The Illustration: How to Merchandise It

When I come back to the prospect, I have something with me that I've made up—something in the way of an *illustration*. My illustration is open face. It looks simple. It *is* simple. But, remember, a lot of work went into making it simple. You just don't throw an illustration together.

Ben, I can see that you've worked out the solution to the person's specific problem in detail. I'm sure you've worked hard to get the right facts and the right figures. What impresses me is that all those facts and figures—well, they don't look dull. They look exciting. How do you do it?

THE BOOK
WHOLE LIFE ILLUSTRATION
Face Amount $ 1,000,000 Sex M Age 50
New York Life Insurance Co. Premiums Paid Annually
Rated Non-Smoker
LEDGER ILLUSTRATION

POLICY DIVIDEND OPTION Paid-Up Additions

YR	NET PREMIUM	POLICY CASH VALUE	DIVIDEND CASH VALUE	NET CASH VALUE	FACE AMOUNT OF ADDS	NET DEATH BENEFIT
1	24040	0	0	0	0	1000000
2	24040	0	3090	3090	0	1000000
3	24040	14000	7967	21967	8636	1008636
4	24040	32000	14868	46868	21502	1021502
5	24040	50000	24146	74146	38774	1038774
6	24040	68000	36000	104000	60881	1060881
7	24040	87000	50660	137660	87806	1087806
8	24040	107000	68347	175347	119590	1119590
9	0	127000	62921	189921	101285	1101285
10	0	147000	58495	210495	86108	1086108
11	0	168000	55444	229444	73960	1078960
12	0	189000	53904	249904	65371	1071371
13	0	217000	54086	279086	60317	1067317
14	0	245000	56206	310206	58914	1066914
15	0	273000	60530	343530	61272	1070272
16	0	301000	67292	379292	67573	1077573
17	0	329000	76678	417678	77923	1088923
18	0	357000	88872	458872	92323	1104323
19	0	385000	103999	502999	110771	1123771
20	0	413000	122310	550310	133163	1147163
---- AGE						
65	0	301000	67292	379292	67573	1077573
70	0	437000	143750	596750	159612	1174612
LE	0	733000	1110809	1868809	1202194	2227194
80	0	647000	623372	1295372	693740	1718740
99	0	1000000	4700755	5725755	4393907	5418907

Policy Prem. of $ 24,040.00 w/ WP of $ 0.00 ADB of $ 0.00 PPO of $ 0.00
-------------- AVERAGE --------------------------------- NET -----------------
Net Death Benefit @ L.E. $ 1,303,031 Net Death Benefit @ L.E. $ 2,227,194
Cost of a Dollar @ L.E. $ .148 Cost of a Dollar @ L.E. $ .086

Dividends are not guaranteed. For explanation refer to form 11939.
This illustration was prepared for New York Life Insurance Co. using ISIS.
Insurance Sales Illustrations Systems is an independent computer software
service company and is not affiliated with any insurer or financial institution.
Page # 1; ISIS Ver. 2.7 Date Prepared 04-08-1988 by BEN FELDMAN CLU

I use good paper. I use good typing equipment. I use color. I give the illustration a name. And I put the person's name on the illustration. An illustration might read: A BONUS POLICY FOR JOHN JONES. Notice the dollar bill. Why is it there? Because my illustrations are bundles of money. I'm selling money.

Learn to merchandise. But don't get carried away; don't let *how* you present the picture complicate the picture. Your illustration must be simple because unless it *is* simple, your prospect won't understand it. And if he or she doesn't understand it—know what happens? He or she won't buy it.

Chapter 26

Never Underestimate a Person's Needs

On that illustration you just showed me, Ben—those figures! That's a lot of money. Don't you find those major amounts hard to sell?

His problem has a price tag. The price tag has to be paid. Either his family pays it with dollars or he pays it with pennies. Which is better? Aren't you helping him? The bigger the price tag, the more you're helping him. He needs that policy. Never underestimate his needs. When you underestimate his needs, you're not helping him. When you think small, you're actually hurting the person you should be helping. Tell him what he needs—no matter how big it looks. Then you're truly helping him.

When I come back, the prospect really doesn't know how much I'm going to bring him. Maybe in his mind he has a picture of $500,000 *now*, but in a year

from now—what will he need? A million. So I come
back with a policy for a million. He doesn't buy the
million—that's too much for him because he can't see
down the road that far. But you know what happens?
He doesn't want the five hundred thousand, and he
doesn't buy the million, but he does take something in
between. You don't wind up with the $500,000, you
don't wind up with the million—you wind up with,
say, $700,000.

*That's a lot of money, Ben. Those are awfully big
figures you throw around. I get tongue-tied when I
have to say to people, "Buy something worth a million dollars." Can you give me some advice?*

Have you ever thought how funny it is that a man
will insure everything he owns for what it's worth—
except his life? He has a car he has insured. For how
much? For pretty much what it's worth. He has a
home he has insured. For how much? For pretty much
what it's worth. The one thing he doesn't insure for
what it's worth is his life. Apparently, it isn't worth
much.

He'll insure his life for only 5 to 10 percent of
what it's worth. The most precious thing in the world,
insured for only 5 to 10 percent of its value! Isn't that
a little crazy? The home is replaceable, the car is
replaceable—but a man's life? In enough time a man
can buy a new car or build a new home—but, tell me,
with all the time in the world, how can he get a new
life?

The *value* of a man or woman's life—why should
you stop thinking big when you think of a person's
life? What's bigger? Do you know of anything that's
bigger? Tell me something: How much is your life
worth? Want to know how much? How much did you

insure it for? Well, *that's* what it's worth—no more, no less. Is your life worth as little as the value you put on it? Can you ever put *too much* value on your life? There are people who are insured for fifty thousand dollars; there are people who are insured for five hundred thousand dollars; there are people who are insured for millions of dollars—but *there is no one insured for more than his life is worth.*

There's no one who will be willing to trade all their tomorrows for their life insurance; there's not a person in the world who'd be willing to do that. Don't be afraid to put a big price tag on a person's life.

You know, you become the most important person in the world when, at the end of a year, you've sold a million dollars worth of insurance. Why? Because as sure as you're sitting there, one million dollars walks in because of what you did. And that one million dollars walks in when a spouse needs it most, when a company needs it most, when a family needs it most.

Ben, I have my own kind of "money fright." I mean it's my prospect who has all that money, not me. That makes it hard for me to sell. What shall I do?

I never had any money as a young man. I was a poor boy. You know what I earned on my first job? Ten dollars a week. I admit the other person's money scared me.

But when I went in to see a man, and he had money, and I didn't have so much money, I said to myself, "You know, tax is a great leveler of income, and just because he's made a hundred thousand—or a hundred million—that doesn't mean that he's got money. The man who makes a little more, spends a little more. The man who makes a little more, pays a little more tax. The man who makes a little more, gives a little more to charity, and so on and so on."

May I ask you: How many men and women with million dollar estates die with only a few thousand dollars in cash in the bank? Money's funny: Sometimes the more you have, the less you have. So when you think of it *that* way, you can walk in feeling that that prospect's money is nothing to be scared of.

Chapter 27

What to Answer When the Prospect Says, "I've Got to Take It Up with ..."

Ben, when you get to the stage of showing figures—
and particularly big figures—doesn't the prospect
almost always say, "I've got to take it up with my ac-
countant or my attorney"? What do you do then?

That's an objection you frequently meet. It can hurt. It can hurt the prospect and it can hurt you. That's because accountants and attorneys tend to delay. They raise objections that put doubts in a person's mind. These people could stop a sale. Let me go over how I handle this type of objection because it's important, very important.

Let's take the accountant. An accountant is a very important person. Tell me, could a businessperson get along without an accountant? The accountant figures out the truth in figures, and she's needed. She says two and two make four; and if you go to the bank and borrow ten thousand dollars, she'll put the ten thou-

sand dollars on the balance sheet, and she'll tell you
that you have a liability of ten thousand dollars. But
will she *pay* the ten thousand dollars? Will she pay
any of the bills? No, she won't. She'll just figure them
up.

But some day there will be debts to pay—to Uncle
Sam or to the bank. She'll figure out the bills that have
to be paid, all right. But when the chips are down, she
won't pay them. She'll figure out the amount of cash
owed. But she can't *create* the cash. Someone has to
pay those bills. Know what I tell the prospect? I tell
him all I've just told you about his accountant, and
then I add:

"The tax must be paid—unless Uncle Sam will
treat you differently from anybody else. Who's going
to pay the tax—the accountant? Somebody has to pay
the tax. And the day it becomes payable, that'll be the
day I walk in with enough money to pay it. I promise
you it *will* get paid! Can your accountant make that
promise?"

Take the lawyer. He's important, too. The business
person needs him. He does a good job, a necessary job.
But be careful. The lawyer can take the case away
from you. A lawyer can stop a case from moving—and
once a case stops moving, the case is dead. What good
is a lawyer unless he finds something wrong? Do you
think he's going to say, "That's a wonderful thing,
Feldman!"

When a woman says to you, "I have to show this
to my lawyer," say to that woman:

"Fine! But what is it that you're going to show to
your lawyer? The only thing I want to do is *create*
money. Can your lawyer do that? Is he an expert in
creating money? Your lawyer is a wonderful person.

You need him. But he doesn't pay the bills. I think we should all stay in our backyards. The lawyer's job—that's to *distribute* money. My job is to do what no one else can do: To *create* money. If I don't create it, he'll have nothing to distribute."

The basic purpose of the life insurance salesperson is to create and not get all wrapped up in something that's the job of the lawyer, the accountant, the banker or someone else. Our job is to create cash, not to distribute it. Make that clear to a prospect.

Chapter 28

The Premium: Never Look for Extra Money

Let's get back to big packages. They mean big premiums. Suppose I make my presentation and the prospect says, "I buy everything you say—but I just don't have the money to buy the policy." Where do I look for that prospect's extra money so he can pay the premiums?

There is no such thing as extra money. None of us has extra money. We make a little more, so we live a little better. We make a little more, so we buy a second car. We make a little more because we want more of the better things of life. We'd like to have a home on the lake; why not? So between buying more and Uncle Sam saying, "Whoa, whoa, I'm your partner. You make a little more, so I want a little more," you'll find most people never having any extra money. And no matter what it is you're selling, *if you look for extra money, you won't find it. Never look for extra money. There isn't any.*

The mistake a lot of us make, you see, is to look for extra money. If you reach down into a person's pocket for his wallet, he'll break your arm.

Chapter 29

Finding the Premium Money: The Family Comes First

If there's no extra money, Ben, how's the prospect able to pay the premiums?

All people, when the chips are down, will put their families first. That's top priority. When I was selling smaller policies, I would say to a prospect:

"You need a system of priorities. First things should come first. Do you want your family to go on living the way you've accustomed them to live? Well, let's look at the picture. They need $50,000 a year to live. Maybe when you're gone, they can get by with $45,000 or $40,000 or some lesser amount. And how much insurance did you say you have? One hundred thousand? Fine, they can live on that for two years, three years at the most. Now, how old is your little boy? Eight years old? Let's say the money will last for three years; how old will he be then? Eleven? Eleven—is that old enough for him to stand on his own feet? Old enough for him to start earning enough to see himself through school and college?"

This could tear a man apart. What I was saying to him was real, very real. I'd say to that man: "One hundred thousand dollars. That's fine. But divide that by time—the time that's necessary to do the things your widow will have to do: Pay off the home, educate the children, meet the medical expenses—time to do a lot of things, make many dreams come true. How much time will $100,000 underwrite?"

He understood he needed more insurance—but he didn't have the money for the premiums. What did he do? He took a little bit from here, a little bit from there. He didn't have any *extra* money, but he *had* money, and he diverted enough of it from other things to pay the premiums. Why? Because he'd established priorities: His family came first.

> *But, Ben, those were small policies—small premiums. It wasn't too hard to find the money. But didn't you find it harder to find the money when you began to sell bigger policies?*

I would say to a prospect: "When you save money in a bank, that's an accumulation. But we *create* money for you. Who else can do that? You may need the money we create. How do you know you have enough time? If you do have enough time, we'll give you your money back. But if you don't have enough time, the money we create will keep your family going. You might not make quite as much money with us as you would investing your money in a bank, but you know what *we're* going to do? We're going to make darned sure that your family has a right to go on living.

"You know, I have $500,000 insurance for my family. You've only got $150,000—and yet you earn as much money as I do, maybe more. You live in a house just as nice as mine. You want the same things for your children as I want for mine. You know what I want for them?

"I want the right to send them to school. An education costs money. Do you think you'll have enough money? If you begin paying for that education now, when your little boy is five years old, you'll have 13 years to pay for it. But if you wait until he's ready for college, will you be ready? If you can't pay for it slowly over a period of years, why do you think you'll be able to pay for it all at once? And you know, the odds will be that when your neighbor's little boy goes to college—yours *won't*."

That shook the prospect up. That made the prospect understand that to find that money for premiums was the first priority. Believe me, he or she found that money.

So what you do when you talk to a person is show them the need to put first things first—to put their family first. Say to a woman who is head of a household:

"Your family has a right to go on living. And living the way you want them to go on living, that costs money. Somebody's got to pay that cost whether you buy the policy or not. There is a cost either way: If you do or if you don't. If you do, you can pay for it with two-cent dollars. If you don't, your family can pay for it by doing without. Doing without *what*? Doing without living in a nice home. Doing without an education for the children. Doing without having the nice things you're so happy to give them."

You hit a person hard, you build a fire under them. So they look for the money to pay the premiums. They'll take the money from savings, investments, maybe they won't drink so many cocktails. They'll spend a little less, but you know what? They'll come up with the premiums.

Ben, what about the field of large estates, close corporations, partnerships—when there's really big money involved—what do you say to a man who says to you, "Sure, Ben, I know I need the policy, but where's the money to come from?"

I say to this person:

"You know, the money has to come from someplace. This policy can't be free. If it were, it wouldn't be much good. But as far as paying the premiums: There's a price tag on doing it; there's a price tag on not doing it. Doing nothing doesn't solve your problem; it only postpones it. You have a right to postpone it. But if you postpone solving your problem, you know who'll have to solve it? Your wife. Only she won't be your wife. She'll be your widow. And your whole family—your son and daughter as well as your wife, because she's going to need help—together, they'll have to do with hundred-cent dollars what you *should* have done with *discounted dollars*. If you have trouble paying pennies on the dollar, do you think your family will have it easy paying what must be paid with full hundred-cent dollars?"

So the appeal is once again: A person's family comes first. Is that right, Ben?

A man or woman doesn't want to see everything he or she has worked a lifetime for go down the drain.

They don't want to see Uncle Sam and other creditors take everything. They don't want the creditors to come first. They want their family to come first. I say:

"I know there isn't any extra money. If you make a lot, you pay out a lot. You spend more, you pay more taxes. I'm in the same boat. But it's a question of some things come first and some things come second. Your creditors should not come first. Your family should not come second. You've spent 30 years putting your estate together. For whom? Your creditors? Or for your family? Do you want to keep what you worked for? Do you want your family to have what is rightfully theirs—everything you worked for?"

Ben, you know I tried this approach, and my prospect said to me, "I agree with everything you said, but can you tell me where I can squeeze, say, four thousand dollars or five thousand dollars out of my till? That money is after taxes—and that's an important consideration. Tell me: Where's the money going to come from to do exactly what you think I should do?" How would I answer that prospect, Ben?

I would say:

"I know there's a big flow of money through your corporation—that's where the money's going to come from. But if three hundred dollars a month makes that much difference, you're already broke and you don't know it."

That stirs a prospect up.

Chapter 30

Take the Premiums from Capital, and Take It Away from the Tax Collector

You just told me how business owners can find the premiums in their corporations. Is there any other way you can help a person find the premiums so they don't have to come out of their current income?

For older people in particular, tell them:

"Don't take the premiums from income, take them from capital. Why? Because when you do that, you take it away from the tax collector."

I have a gentleman in mind who's paying $30,000 a year in premiums—and that's a pretty good chunk of money. You know, this man could pay that money out of income, but why should he? He'd still have to pay income taxes on it.

I have lots of clients who take their premiums out of capital.

Chapter 31

Dividends: Use Them to Expand Coverage

Is there any other specific source of money
for premiums?

When I prospect, I check the person to see if he has a policy. Sometimes he has. Sometimes the *dividends have mounted up. There's* the money! I say to this prospect:

"Look, we already have the money. If you leave it the way it is, you have $15,000 piled up in dividends. But put that $15,000 to work with me, and if something happens, we'll pay the claim *and* give you back the $15,000."

Once they buy a policy, most people pay little attention to it. They pay attention to paying the premiums, yes. But they usually pay no attention to dividends. Once a year, when the premium comes due, they pay it—and that's it. And then they forget about the policy for another year. Dividends quite often are left to accumulate. *And it's from dividends that I find that I can begin new policies.* So I tell a prospect:

"We've already got your money. All we have to do is make sure that you're still eligible for it. Suppose I put it together and you take a look. All we need is medical underwriting. I'll set up an exam, and we'll go from there."

I had a case where a man had built up substantial coverage over the years and had accumulated a large number of dollars in dividends. One day I said to this man:

"Lou, you know something? Your program is a bit out of balance. We've done a good job in regard to your part of the program. But you know, you have a marital deduction, which means that your estate will be tax-free only because it goes to your wife. But what happens then? While the money isn't taxable in *your* estate, it will be taxable in *her* estate. So why don't we create a little better balance in your overall program. *Why not use some of the dividends that have accumulated—that are continuing to be earned on your overall program—to set up a policy for her?*"

He liked the idea. I had her examined. The policy was issued. It was the simplest sale in the world. Know why? *I already had the money for the premiums.*

I had another case along these lines. I had the woman examined, and there had been some changes, and we turned her down. Meanwhile, a lot of dividends had piled up. She had almost $30,000 in dividend accumulations and between $6,000 and $8,000 in annual dividends coming in each year. I couldn't insure this woman. But you know what I did? I insured her son. Instead of writing the mother $200,000, I wrote the son $500,000! *The dividends on the mother's insurance*—dividends that had accumulated, dividends that will be earned each year—*those dividends pay the premiums on the son's insurance.* Simplest sale in the world!

There are dozens of sales like these that you can pick up. Say to a prospect:

"I can expand your coverage by 25 percent, and you don't have to take a cent out of your pocket. I already have the money. Let me put it together and you take a look."

Another way to make use of the dividends that have piled up in a client's policy is to use those dividends to pay the premiums on that policy. In so doing, you have freed up premium dollars that can be used to purchase new coverage. Since the client will already be accustomed to paying out these premium dollars, there can be very little objection to continuing the payments.

PART 2

Chapter 32

How to Create Packages with Big Price Tags

You call yourself a "package salesman." Ben, can you give me some guidelines on how I can create packages with big price tags?

The packages you create are *real*. They're made to fit *real* problems. They're made to solve problems. *Serious* problems. Serious—why? Because either the prospects have to pay or their families have to pay.

When you're creating a package, your imagination has to be in high gear. You work *first* with your imagination—it's got to be in your *mind* first—then you work with words and facts and figures.

I'm a young man just starting. Can I go after the larger policies?

You see where you're going to stub your toe: You're not quite ready to talk about the big policy from the standpoint of tax impact on the estate, of finding dollars to pay what must be paid. Are you familiar with what takes place when a person walks out—the tax impact? Have you studied the estate table to know how much it will be?

As a young man, you must pay the price in study, and you must be able to take the problem apart to understand what makes and creates a problem today and tomorrow. It isn't that difficult to do. It takes time—but what doesn't take time? If you're willing to do that, then you can do so much good for so many people.

What are the areas I must study up on to sell
larger policies?

Most of my problems arise from close corporations, partnerships, and family-held companies. I build my packages around a few fundamental problems because these problems have big price tags. These problems concern: Estate taxes, company continuity, income taxes, guaranteed markets, keypeople, corporate credit, and similar areas. Later on, I'll answer your questions about them in some detail.

How long would it take me to learn how to sell a
larger package?

If you work at it, spending some time every day on basic background as it involves tax structure and the life insurance contract, I would say that within a year you will have acquired a basic background that will permit you to go out and do this kind of work.

Are there any courses I should take?

I don't know where you could go other than to your own company for the sort of information you're looking for. When you get into a case, go to your manager and tell him what you have in mind. Let him go to the advanced underwriting department in your home office to help you put the case together. They're familiar with cases involving major amounts. They know how to do it.

There are agents in your company who are doing it. Go out with an agent like that on a case or two. On your first case or so, why not give that agent the commission, and she'll give you the know-how and the procedure? Then do it yourself.

Work at it, and it will work. Instead of writing 50 cases at $10,000 apiece—that's a half-million dollars—write 1 case at a million dollars.

You know something, the big man with the big problem is easier to sell than the small man with the small problem. That's because the big man is accustomed to using banks and corporate credit lines; he's not taking the money out of his own pocket. He's using the corporate pocketbook. He doesn't hesitate to have the corporation buy something if it's the right thing to do. The bank won't object to putting up the money either, because that money is going to keep the company strong.

Prove to yourself what I'm telling you. Jump in. Get your feet wet. You may stub your toe a time or two in the beginning, but you'll become stronger for it. It *will* work. Your cases *will* get bigger and bigger and bigger. They'll get *even* bigger if you remember to *look down the road.* The client grows, the company grows, the problem grows.

That's how you create bigger cases with major amounts. I like this sort of work. To me, it's not real work. I start and I don't stop!

Ben, can you give me a very brief example of how
you create a case?

I spend hour after hour creating a case, making it logical, then making it simple. For example, I know someone with an estate worth roughly $8 million. When that person goes, the estate tax will take about half of that $8 million. It's very difficult to pull $4 million out of $8 million without wrecking that person's company. It leaves a big hole. I say:

"Do it my way. The premium on a $4 million policy is about $10,000 a month. The interest on a $4 million loan is over $30,000 a month. If you pay an amount equal to about one third the interest charge, we'll pay the principal. If you don't do it my way, you'll have to do it your way."

Make it logical. Then make it simple. When you do, you'll sell it.

Chapter 33

Study Estates: The Price Tags Reach Seven Figures

What made you turn to the problems of estates to write policies involving major amounts?

I began to study estates. Study them and you'll find that in estates of a hundred thousand dollars, of a million dollars, of ten million dollars, there is almost no money—no cash. The people who accumulate these estates have all kinds of other assets, such as stock, buildings, machinery, land, but they don't have much cash. And it's only money that Uncle Sam wants when these people die.

The day a person walks out, Uncle Sam walks in and asks for the government's share. Could you, right now, pay out what you might owe? It's simply not feasible to carry the amount of cash required to pay inheritance taxes on large estates. But the day you walk out, the government walks in, and they want cash. Furthermore, they have a way of getting it.

Where's the cash to come from? *From* the estate? That's *forced* liquidation. Liquidation of assets while a man is here is one thing, but after he's gone, it may be entirely different. It may not be an "*orderly*" liquidation. When a buyer knows the widow has to sell— isn't the buyer going to offer a low price? Somebody may get the assets for one-half of what they're worth. A person must either create cash to absorb the tax impact or the tax impact will absorb the estate.

The function of life insurance is to create cash. I usually say:

"It's better to use insurance to pay your estate taxes. While you might pay $500,000 tax, you'll pay very little for the $500,000. And your estate remains intact."

Chapter 34

How to Conduct an Estate Interview

Ben, I wonder if you can give me the highlights of an estate interview?

I might open by saying:

"Very nice of you to see me. You know, Mr. Jones, you've been running pretty hard now for about 30 years, and in spite of the tax structure, you've built a beautiful estate. Now I presume you built this estate for your family. May I show you what happens in most estates?"

Here's what I show him:

WILLIAM WOODWARD, JR.
Prominent Sportsman and Financier
Oyster Bay, New York

Died October 30, 1955, at age 35

Gross Estate $11,063,946

Total Costs   7,443,494

Net Estate .... $ 3,620,452

Cash in Estate, $553,041

OVER 67% SHRINKAGE

SETTLEMENT COSTS

Debts	$ 543,869
Admn. Expense	241,628
Attorney's Fee	350,000
Executor's Fee	439,211
N.Y. Estate Tax	1,206,725
*Federal Estate Tax ..	4,662,061
TOTAL COSTS	$7,443,494

Debts Day
Before Death

DEFICIT $6.890.000

*No marital deduction.

DWIGHT D. EISENHOWER
34th U.S. President
Gettysburg, Pennsylvania

Died March 28, 1969, at age 78

Gross Estate $2,905,857
Total Costs 671,429

Net Estate $2,234,428

Cash in Estate, $60,820

SETTLEMENT COSTS

Debts	$140,036
Admn. Expense	21,853 (1)
Attorney's Fee	68,900
Executor's Fee	30,500
Pa. Inheritance Tax	42,026
*Federal Estate Tax	368,114
TOTAL COSTS	$671,429

Debts Due Before Death

DEFICIT $610.000

*Full marital deduction.

* Full marital deduction. Widow has life estate from Trust Funds. These figures are only first and partial accounting filed to date.

(1) Includes over $6,500 to run farm until crops harvested and sold.

OVER 23% SHRINKAGE

© Estate Research Company 1973, P. O. Box 2157, Castro Valley, California 94546

JOHN F. JELKE

Chairman, John F. Jelke Co., Oleomargarine Manufacturers
Chicago, Illinois

Died January 1, 1965, at age 77

Gross Estate $6,971,664
Total Costs 3,778,519

Net Estate $3,193,145

Cash in Estate, $227,856

Included in the gross estate is $115,000 of life insurance.

OVER 54% SHRINKAGE

● 1973 Estate Research Company, P.O. Box 2157, Castro Valley, California 94546

SETTLEMENT COSTS

Debts	$ 4,902
Admn. Expense	179,376
Attorney's Fee	140,000
Executor's Fee	140,000
Ill. Inheritance Tax ...	549,870
*Federal Estate Tax ...	2,764,371
TOTAL COSTS	**$3,778,519**

Debts Day Before Death

DEFICIT $3,551,000

*No marital deduction; no spouse surviving.

HUMPHREY BOGART

PROMINENT ACTOR

Humphrey Bogart was born in New York City, the son of Dr. Belmont de Forest and Maud (Humphrey) Bogart. According to Who's Who in the Theatre he was born on January 23, 1899; according to the Warner Brothers Publicity Department he was born on December 25, 1900 ("but demands birthday presents as well as Christmas presents"). His father was a prominent New York surgeon and his mother was interested in art.

Bogart got his first acting part in 1920 with a road company and he made his first appearance on a New York stage in 1922. For the next thirteen years Bogart played roles of various dimensions in a long succession of plays. Some were successes, some did moderately well, others were out and out failures; but Bogart was rarely unemployed. Bogart took a number of screen tests before he landed a motion picture role and was actually in motion pictures commencing in 1930.

Motion picture critics, as well as the less critical motion picture going public, found Bogart an exceptionally competent actor. He told reporters that "all I do to look evil is to let my beard grow for two days", but critics thought he was merely being modest. He could drop his accurate English and fall into the clipped jargon of the underworld; he could snarl or cringe, be suave or crudely sinister, and all apparently without effort.

DIED JANUARY 14, 1957, AGE 57

Gross Estate ....$910,146.

Total Settlement Costs .... 274,234.

Net Estate ....$635,912.

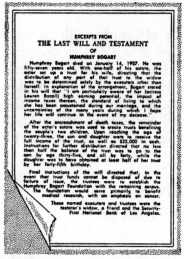

EXCERPTS FROM
THE LAST WILL AND TESTAMENT
OF
HUMPHREY BOGART

Humphrey Bogart died on January 14, 1957. He was fifty-seven years old. With one-half of his estate, the actor set up a trust for his wife, directing that the distribution of any part of that trust to the widow was to be determined solely by the executors other than herself. In explanation of the arrangement, Bogart stated in his will that "I am particularly aware of her (actress Lauren Bacall) high earning potential, the impact of income taxes thereon, the standard of living to which she has been accustomed during our marriage, and the uncertainties of the many years during which I hope her life will continue in the event of my decease."

After the encroachment of death taxes, the remainder of the actor's estate was used to create trusts benefiting the couple's two children. Upon reaching the age of twenty-three, the son and daughter were to receive the full income of the trust, as well as $25,000 in cash. Instructions for further distribution directed that no less than half the balance of the trust was to go to the son by age thirty-five, and all by ferry, while the daughter was to have obtained at least half of her trust by her forty-fifth birthday.

Final instructions of the will directed that, in the event that trust funds cannot be disposed of due to failure of issue, the trustees were to establish the Humphrey Bogart Foundation with the remaining corpus. The foundation would serve primarily to benefit medical research, with an emphasis on cancer.

These named executers and trustees were the testator's widow, a friend and the Security-First National Bank of Los Angeles.

The Settlement Costs:

Debts	$101,767
Administration Expense	3,988
Attorney's Fee	11,249
Executor's Fee	11,249
California Inheritance Tax	21,325
Federal Estate Tax*	124,655
TOTAL SETTLEMENT COSTS	$274,234

*50% Marital Deduction

Cash in estate $25,693

Now what are they? They are taken from actual probate records. I pick out those that I think will have impact—names people will recognize—and I say to the prospect:

"May I show you what happens to millionaires? You may recognize names because these cases are authentic. Look what happened in this case. The executor went out and borrowed $150,000 to prevent a forced liquidation.

"Look at another one here. Do you remember Humphrey Bogart the actor? Look what happened. He had everything—except money. Now, he didn't owe a lot of money. Lots of people die owing almost nothing, but the next day they owe hundreds of thousands of dollars—maybe millions of dollars. They call it taxes.

"Here is James A. Dooley of Chicago, Illinois. He had a $13 million estate. How much did he owe the day before he died? Two million dollars. How much cash did he have? Two million dollars. But the day after he died, he owed $6 million. How did the estate get the cash it needed to pay the bills? They have a name for this. You know what they call it? Liquidation."

JAMES A. DOOLEY

Illinois Supreme Court Justice, Chicago, Illinois

			SETTLEMENT COSTS		
Gross Estate		$13,275,170			
Total Costs	$6,215,367	6,228,367	Debts		$1,877,387
			Administration Expense		31,700
Net Estate	$7,059,803	$ 7,046,803	Attorney's Fee		285,000
	Cash in Estate, $1,812,539		Executor's Fee		Waived
Included in the gross estate is			Illinois Inheritance Tax		1,043,872
$62,500 of life insurance			*Federal Estate Tax	$2,977,408	2,990,408
			TOTAL COSTS	$6,215,367	$6,228,367

*33⅓% marital deduction

The man I'm talking to has done what most others do: Made a lot of money and locked it up in one thing or another. He has no ready cash to pay the government. You show him what happened to so and so, and to so and so, and you build a fire beneath him.

How do you show a person the effect of the tax impact on his or her own estate?

I present an Estate Tax Table in color that shows him how much of what he owns isn't his and a discounted dollar illustration showing mathematically that he can buy dollars for pennies each.

I say:

"Let me show you the part of your estate that isn't yours." And that part could be in six figures or in seven figures. "Could you write me a check for that amount without it hurting a little bit? I'm not saying it'll break your company, but wouldn't it bend it?

"So why do you want to run hard for 30 years and then have 15 years go down the drain? You know, there's a price if you do something or if you don't do something. Most estates, some day, fall apart—not because you did something wrong, but because you did nothing; that's what's wrong."

I can see the logic of your approach. The man wants to know what he can do to keep his estate from falling apart, and you tell him how he can do it with discounted dollars. Is that right?

Yes, he doesn't want to see his estate fall apart. I show him that it *will* fall apart if he doesn't take action *now* because if he waits too long—the man is getting on in years—he won't be able to get insurance. I say to this man:

JOHN DOE
VHOLE LIFE ILLUSTRATION
Face Amount $ 1,000,000 Sex M Age 50
New York Life Insurance Co. Premiums Paid Annually
Rated Non-Smoker
LEDGER ILLUSTRATION

POLICY DIVIDEND OPTION Paid-Up Additions

YR	NET PREMIUM	POLICY CASH VALUE	DIVIDEND CASH VALUE	NET CASH VALUE	FACE AMOUNT OF ADDS	NET DEATH BENEFIT
1	24040	0	0	0	0	1000000
2	24040	0	3090	3090	0	1000000
3	24040	14000	7967	21967	8636	1008636
4	24040	32000	14868	46868	21502	1021502
5	24040	50000	24146	74146	38774	1038774
6	24040	68000	36000	104000	60881	1060881
7	24040	87000	50660	137660	87806	1087806
8	24040	107000	68347	175347	119590	1119590
9	0	127000	62921	189921	101285	1101285
10	0	147000	58495	210495	86108	1086108
11	0	168000	55444	229444	73960	1078960
12	0	189000	53904	249904	65371	1071371
13	0	217000	54086	279086	60317	1067317
14	0	245000	56206	310206	58914	1066914
15	0	273000	60530	343530	61272	1070272
16	0	301000	67292	379292	67573	1077573
17	0	329000	76678	417678	77923	1088923
18	0	357000	88872	458872	92323	1104323
19	0	385000	103999	502999	110771	1123771
20	0	413000	122310	550310	133163	1147163
---- AGE						
65	0	301000	67292	379292	67573	1077573
70	0	437000	143750	596750	159612	1174612
75	0	548000	313840	882840	356212	1376212
80	0	647000	623372	1295372	693740	1718740
99	0	1000000	4700755	5725755	4393907	5418907

Policy Prem. of $ 24,040.00 w/ WP of $ 0.00 ADB of $ 0.00 PPO of $ 0.00
-------------- AVERAGE --------------------------------- NET ------------------
Net Death Benefit 20th yr $ 1,071,059 Net Death Benefit 20th yr $ 1,147,163
Cost of a Dollar 20th yr $ .18 Cost of a Dollar 20th yr. $ .168

"Mr. Jones, the taxes must be paid *from* your estate—or *for* your estate. Let me pay it *for* your estate—with discounted dollars. Pulling the amount of cash the tax collector wants out of the estate leaves a hole in the estate—quite often a big hole—so big a lot of things fall apart. It's better to use insurance to pay the tax collector than take it out of the estate. While you might pay two hundred thousand dollars in tax, you'll pay very little for the two hundred thousand dollars.

"So put me on the payroll. I'll work for four hundred dollars a month. The day you walk out, two hundred thousand dollars walks in. And while you're paying premiums, you're piling up cash. When you need it, you can get it."

Yes, I say, "Put me on your payroll." Just exactly that. Most companies are accustomed to putting people on the payroll. One person more or less doesn't make much difference. You know, you could be the most important person on his payroll—because the day he walks out, you walk in with enough cash to pay everything that must be paid.

How do you close, Ben?

I might say to this man:

"Mr. Jones, part of what you own isn't yours. It belongs to the tax collector. And yet if an estate is worth building, it's worth keeping. Even though you paid income tax all your life, part of what you have left still isn't yours. And the day you walk out, Uncle Sam walks in, and he'll want a great big chunk of your estate. Furthermore, he has a way of getting it. You have a problem; if you don't do something about it, if you don't solve it, you simply postpone it; some day, someone will have to do something about it. If you can qualify, I've got discounted dollars—dollars for pennies apiece. My dollars cost roughly 2¢ or 3¢ per dollar per year. It'll take a long time to pay in the amount we guarantee to pay out. I'm sure you don't want the tax load falling on your family. Let's use my plan. Suppose I put it together and you take a look."

Chapter 35

A Special Sales Aid for the Estate Interview

Ben, I've heard you say that the purpose of a sales aid is to get the prospect's attention. If you get the prospect's attention, you're better able to make a sale. Your tax tables and your probate charts certainly get attention and start the prospect thinking as well. Do you use any other sales aids in your estate interview?

Occasionally, I'll take two unsigned checks out of my pocket and show them to the prospect. One check is payable to Internal Revenue Service for $500,000 and the other check is payable to my company for $1,000. I'll say:

"Some day you or your executor is going to sign one of these checks. Which one, Ms. Prospect?"

Sometimes I hand her the $500,000 check and ask her to sign it. Naturally, she hesitates. Then I hand her the check for $1,000.

"Just sign the little one," I say, "and I'll sign the big one."

Chapter 36

How to Handle Multi-Million-Dollar Estate Problems

What puzzles me is that people with multi-million-dollar estates don't know enough to get insurance protection. Don't they have advisors?

This man was a senator. A very wealthy man. A large part of his assets was wrapped up in an oil company. You would think that such a man would have access to good counsel, wouldn't you? Working with attorneys, working with auditors all the time he should have good guidance, you'd think. But one day he died, and the taxes came to nine million dollars. And there wasn't any money. I wouldn't say he had good counsel, would you?

Where was the nine million dollars to come from? Who in the world with an estate of about twenty million, has half of it lying around loose? Where can an estate get that kind of money without liquidating

SENATOR ROBERT S. KERR
U.S. Senator, Oklahoma City, Oklahoma
Died January 1, 1963
Gross Estate Approximately $20,000,000

THE TULSA TRIBUNE   MARCH 31, 1964

$9.4 MILLION DUE

Taxes Will Take About Half of Kerr's Estate

From the State Capital
Bureau of The Tribune

OKLAHOMA CITY—Federal and state inheritance taxes will take almost half of the late Sen. Robert S. Kerr's $20.8 milion estate, it developed today.

Executors of the estate have advised the county court $9.4 million in inheritance taxes are due Wednesday and it will be necessary to raise $6.1 million to pay the tax bill.

The executors, Dean A. McGee, president of Kerr-McGee Oil Industries Inc., and Robert S. Kerr Jr., asked for permission to borrow the money needed and pledge the assets of the estate as security.

LOANS OF $1.6 MILLION from the Liberty National Bank of Oklahoma City and of $4.5 million from the First National Bank of Chicago are planned.

In their petition, the executors assert that sale of Kerr-McGee stock—which makes up two-thirds of the estate—would depress the market and cause a substantial loss to the estate.

Largest single item in the estate of the senator, who died in Washington Jan. 1, 1963, of a heart attack, was block of 449,882 shares of stock in Kerr-McGee Oil Industries, Inc. valued at $14,-472,703.

Kerr's will left his estate in trusts for the benefit of his wife and children.

Senator Robert S. Kerr's will was written in 1939 and was never up-dated to take advantage of the marital deduction provisions of the present Federal Estate Tax laws. While attorneys had prepared a revised will, the Senator apparently never took time to sign it.

The result is that Senator Kerr's estate, which means his widow and children, will have to pay almost $9,500,000 in Federal and State Estate Taxes alone, plus substantial administration expenses. The executors have already borrowed over $6,000,000 to pay these estate taxes, which were due April 1, 1964.

Proper estate planning could have saved this estate over $4,000,000.

© ESTATE RESEARCH CO.

SENATOR ROBERT S. KERR
United States Senator
Oklahoma City, Oklahoma

Died January 1, 1963, at age 66

Gross Estate $20,800,000
Total Costs 9,840,000

Net Estate $10,960,000
Cash in Estate, $113,000.

SETTLEMENT COSTS

Debts .... $Unknown (1)
Admn. Expense .... Borne by Heirs
Attorney's Fee 220,000
Executor's Fee 220,000
Okla. Estate Tax and
*Federal Estate Tax ... 9,400,000
TOTAL COSTS $9,840,000

*33 1/3% Marital Deduction

OVER 47% SHRINKAGE

(1) The exact gross estate has not been determined due to complexity of valuations. The executors petitioned the Probate Court for permission to borrow $6,100,000 from two banks to help pay estate taxes rather than sell shares of Kerr-McGee Oil Industries, Inc. stock (449,882 shares valued at $14,472,703) which would have depressed the market and caused substantial loss to the estate.

Under Will the widow was given a life estate in one-sixth of the estate left for her in trust. She renounced the Will and chose to take as a forced heir as if decedent died intestate, all as provided by Oklahoma law, thereby taking one-third of entire estate.

something? There was a lot of stock, but the executors were concerned about depressing the value of the stock so much that the estate—everybody—would suffer, so they decided not to sell the stock. What did they do? They went to a bank and luckily were able to borrow 'six million dollars. But they had to have nine million dollars. They were able to find the additional three million in cash.

The interest on the six million amounted to about $420,000 a year. The senator was around the 60-year mark, and the premium on a policy would have been about $60 per thousand, or about 6 percent. Six percent on six million dollars would have been about $360,000 per year. So by borrowing, the estate paid $420,000 not $360,000. And the estate had to pay the six million dollars back as well.

These things can happen, and they *do* happen.

Had you been able to show the senator his problem, would he probably have solved it your way?

Yes, but he solved his problem by postponing it.

Could you give me a case history of a person you got to before he or she postponed the decision too long?

Here's a case I'm actually working on now. I have a man who's spent all his lifetime becoming wealthy. Now he has an estate that runs into eight figures. The reason the estate grew that big is that this man has the ability to make money make money. He's still doing it. That means the money is not lying around in the form of dollars; it's wrapped up in something. Now someone's going to have to unwrap it when the man walks out and Uncle Sam walks in. The executors won't have a lot of time to do it; under the tax law they have only nine months. The executors may not be able to liquidate with a great loss, so I'm going to go back to see this 70-year-old man.

I think he needs roughly $4 million to pay what has to be paid from an estate standpoint. I'm going to make up a check for $30,000 payable to New York Life; that represents a premium. I'm going to make up another check for $4 million; that represents a problem. The $4 million check will be signed by New York Life and be made payable to his company.

I won't ask him to sign the $30,000 check. I'll ask his company to sign it. It won't even be a personal obligation on his shoulders. I'll ask *him* for nothing. I'll show the man that if his company doesn't sign that $30,000 monthly check, they'll have to borrow. They'll be signing a $30,000 interest check, and they'll still have to repay the $4 million.

Where's the company to get that $30,000 each month? There's a tremendous flow of cash going through big companies every month. Look at a company doing $12 million in sales. That's a million a month flowing through that company. It isn't difficult for that company to sign a check for $1,000 a month or $10,000 a month or even $30,000 a month.

Suppose the man dies three years from now. The company will have paid in roughly one million. It will collect four million, a gain of three million! And no income tax! The company would have to earn six million to duplicate that gain!

Using insurance to protect an estate from falling apart seems so obvious that it's hard to believe anybody could say "no" to you, Ben. But I'm sure it happens. Could you tell me about a case when somebody did say "no"—and how you handled it?

I have another case. She's a woman about 70. I heard some months ago that her husband had died. When she lost him, she lost her right to what we call a "marital deduction," which is the right to transfer her estate to him without paying the tax. So there'll be a lot of tax when she walks out.

I called on her. But she didn't want life insurance. She had a three million dollar estate, but she didn't want life insurance. She could make more money with her money by putting it somewhere else, she said. She wouldn't talk to me or see me after that. Either she was on the phone or at a meeting—there was always some excuse.

So I left her a little package. I gave it to her through her personal secretary. In the package was a tax table. Also included was a probate record and an actual illustration on a million-dollar policy. I also put a little note that I had written to her in the package. What did the note say? Something along these lines:

"All your life you've made decisions. You've tried to make good ones. You've succeeded, and now you may have a very substantial estate. Here's another decision. It's a good one. Let us pay the tax. If you will give us the interest, we will pay the tax. A million–dollar policy costs 7 percent per year. Just seven percent. Why do you want to throw a million dollars away? How long did it take you to earn a million dollars? You probably had to earn two million to keep one million. Ms. Jones, all your life you've exercised good judgment. So why not now? My dollars cost pennies apiece. Yours will cost two dollars apiece. Why not use mine?"

Did this note get you in to see the woman?

It will. She'll see me. She's a very shrewd business-woman and if there's a chance to make a dollar to save a dollar she'll be very interested. We're talking about a million dollars. Her money or my money. She can get my plan and I'll pay the million dollars. If she can't get my money, she'll pay the million dollars. "Ms. Jones, do you want to take a million dollars out of your estate? It's one-third of your lifetime—don't you care?" When I see her, I'll close the sale.

Chapter 37

The Estate Case Illustration: It Looks down the Road to Bigger Sales

Could you show me one or two typical illustrations to demonstrate the estate problem?

Here are a couple of illustrations:

DOLLARS TO DISCOUNT YOUR ESTATE TAX

FOR MR. AND MRS. JOHN DOE

ASSUMES FULL MARITAL DEDUCTION

ESTATE OF - $5,000,000
MARITAL DEDUCTION - $5,000,000

	TODAY	IN 8 YEARS	TOTAL TAX
	JOHN DOE	JANE DOE	
NET ESTATE	$ 0	$9,250,000*	
1. Federal Tax -	$ 0	$3,217,000	$3,217,000
2. State Inheritance Tax -	$398,000	$ 962,000	$1,360,000
3. Administration Costs (approximately 6%) -	$300,000	$ 555,000	$ 855,000
4. Miscellaneous Items (Income Tax accrued, etc.) -	$ 50,000	$ 92,500	$ 142,500
CASH REQUIRED -	$748,000	$4,826,500	$5,574,500

TOTAL CASH REQUIRED - $5,574,500

LOSS OF MARITAL DEDUCTION WILL INCREASE TAX ON FIRST ESTATE.

*Assumes 8% Growth.

Ben Feldman, C.L.U.

DOLLARS TO DISCOUNT YOUR ESTATE TAX

FOR MR. AND MRS. JOHN DOE

ASSUMES USE OF TRUST

ESTATE OF - $5,000,000
MARITAL DEDUCTION - $2,500,000

	TODAY	IN 8 YEARS	TOTAL
	JOHN DOE	JANE DOE	TAX
	$2,500,000	$4,600,000*	
1. Federal Tax -	$ 0	$1,446,900	$1,446,900
2. State Inheritance Tax -	$ 398,000	$ 354,000	$ 752,000
3. Administration Costs (approximately 6%) -	$ 300,000	$ 276,000	$ 576,000
4. Miscellaneous Items (Income Tax accrued, etc.) -	$ 50,000	$ 46,000	$ 96,000
CASH REQUIRED -	$ 748,000	$2,122,900	$2,870,900

TOTAL CASH REQUIRED - $2,870,900

LOSS OF MARITAL DEDUCTION WILL INCREASE TAX ON FIRST ESTATE.

*Assumes 8% Growth.

Ben Feldman, C.L.U.

*Are there any variations on the estate illustrations,
or are they all very much alike?*

I would say that they're all very much alike. The
tax structure is pretty specific. The illustrations are
governed by the size of the estate.

*I notice that in both the illustrations you've shown
me, you're looking down the road.*

If you figure there will be growth, and if you project the rate of growth for another five years, another
ten years, then the estate can double.

*Suppose a person is 70 years old. You won't be pro-
jecting that estate much farther, will you?*

Life expectancy tables would give that person possibly ten more years.

*And you project that far and calculate that the
estate will continue to grow until then?*

Assuming it does, and taking a very conservative
figure—just assume it'll grow 8 percent—ten years down
the road the estate will have doubled.

*So, then, every one of your illustrations will always
be looking down the road as far as the estate
problem is concerned?*

Yes, I might say:

"Ms. Smith, you're 40 and your company is now
worth $1 million. Your company is going to grow, and
when you're 50, it will be worth $2 million. When
you're 60 it will be worth $4 million. Your life expec-
tancy is about 40 years. When you're 80, your com-

pany will be worth about $15 million. If you wait until then to guarantee the cash you'll have to pay Uncle Sam, it'll be too late. Because even if you could get up the premiums, their cost would be prohibitive. But you can do it now.

"You don't have any money? Well, just take an option on it now. That's term insurance. Let's do this. Let's set up $500,000 in permanent coverage and an additional $1 million in term coverage. If you wait, you may become completely uninsurable. If you wait and you get the policy, you won't pay less; you'll always pay more. Take a life insurance policy and study the costs: the sooner you buy, the better."

Here's another example:

A man 38. An estate of five million dollars. I'm looking down the road. At age 48, his estate is going to double. At age 58, it'll be five times what it is today. But *today*, he can buy dollars for 10 cents. You know what that will cost him at age 58? *Thirty cents!*

"So why not buy it now, Mr. Jones? You're better off buying it sooner than later."

Chapter 38

Selling the Million-Dollar Policy

What I'm going to try to do this month is create cases that range from one million to possibly eight million. What I'm going to try to do is arrange for a medical examination. I'll see the prospect and present the problem and say, "I'd like to put it together and you take a look. All I need now is to make sure that you're insurable."

Are these cold cases or are they cases for clients that are already in your files?

Seventy-five percent of these cases are policyholders. As a rule, you can't go out from scratch and write a policy for a million dollars. There's something called "confidence"—the person has to buy a little piece of you. While he may not understand you completely, he must be sure in his mind that you're thinking of him. He senses that you're knowledgeable and that you know what you're doing, that you do have a solution. He knows you're not backing him into a corner for a decision. Never do that because he'll not give you a decision or he'll not give you the right one. So, "Let me put it together...." Ask him for nothing—just time.

How do you sell a million-dollar policy to someone not in your files?

I have a case I'm working on for someone in her mid-thirties. She is already a wealthy young woman. We have a million-dollar contract with a premium of only $1,000 a month. The $1,000 a month will be a corporate payment. For a corporation that runs into many millions, $1,000 a month isn't even petty cash; it isn't a load for the corporation.

The contract is guaranteed to make a million dollars. You know why? We have a very special rider attached to the contract that states, in essence. "We'll give you back your money—and a million besides."

How can we do this?

"Because, Ms. Smith, as you pay in premiums, you pile up cash. The rider in the contract adds enough term insurance to cover the cash. If you were paying $1,000 a month—that's $12,000 a year—20 years later, you will have in roughly a quarter of a million dollars, and the cash value will be half a million dollars. You wrap your car around a tree, or get on the wrong airplane, and something happens to you—what we do is first pay the cash value, which is about double the premium. You never put in the amount you're going to get out. It has to make a million dollars."

So that's the package—a very simple package.

Ben, I would think you have many cases in your files where a client is growing. His estate isn't worth a million now, but he's growing—you can see that—and one day his estate taxes will come to a million. I'm sure you're looking down the road. How do you sell such a person?

If an individual needs a million dollars or more when he dies, he *does* have a problem! Here's what I say:

"How would you like to be a millionaire? Put me on your payroll for $100 a day—and the day you walk out, one million dollars walks in. *Plus* about 75 percent of the amount you paid in. Let me put it together. . . ."

Or I might say:

"We've just put $1 million into an escrow account and have written your name on it. If you'll put me on your payroll for $2,000 a month, someday I'll pay your company $1 million. Your estate will have to pay $1 million for the tax, but your company won't have to pay much for the $1 million. Let me put it together. . . ."

Chapter 39

When the Corporation is the Bulk of the Estate

How do you handle the estate problem when a prospect's corporation is the bulk of the estate?

I say to the prospect: "You could pull money out of your corporation and give it to Uncle Sam and maybe not wreck your company. It wouldn't break it, but it would bend it. You just cannot pull that kind of money out of a corporation without leaving a hole some place.

"You know, there's an easier way of doing it. A person goes along and works and works and works, makes money, and then spends the money. And in a case like yours, you keep plowing it back into the corporation. Why? The corporation is growing. It's getting bigger: More land, more receivables, more inventory, more this, more that, more everything under the sun. And because you're doing this, it *is* getting bigger and bigger. After a while, it's the biggest thing you've got. And because it represents the bulk of your estate, it creates the estate problem.

"Even Uncle Sam recognized this and some years ago revised a section of the Revenue Code, and now the corporation can pay your tax. But the corporation had better have the money. So the insurance industry designed a contract that creates the cash.

"It's so simple. You do nothing. Your company sets up a special account and puts $100 a day into it. My company sets up a special account, and we put $1 million into it. Some day we simply trade accounts. Let me put it together. . . ."

What I was trying to get this prospect to buy was nothing but a Split Dollar Contract.

Did your client deduct the premium as a business expense or corporation expense?

No. There is no way to deduct it.

There isn't? You said it was a close corporation.

There is no method of deducting the premiums. Not unless the client picks it up as income. That's not what we're trying to do.

I see. The corporation does not place coverage on your client as part of his or her compensation.

That's right. If the corporation wants to buy a policy and pay the premium, but vest ownership of the policy in the insured, certainly. But the insured must pick up the premium as additional compensation.

What I'm trying to do is to get the corporation to buy a policy of $1 million. On whose life? On my client's life. They own it. They pay for it. They collect the proceeds. They do not deduct the premiums. But they do *not* pay tax on the proceeds; and I promise you the proceeds will exceed the premiums. Then, under Section 303, the descendent's executor can redeem enough of his or her stock by selling it back to the corporation to pull this money back out. The executor can pull it out without tax consequence of any kind and pay the entire cost of settling the estate.

There are a lot of variations you can get into in the Split Dollar Plan. There are a lot of things you can do. But, basically, I have in mind nothing more than a very simple little contract owned by the corporation.

Chapter 40

How to Sell a Package That Guarantees Company Continuity

I say to a prospect:

"There's a price tag on everything. A person spends a lifetime making money, plowing it back into a successful corporation, becomes quite wealthy, worth a lot of money, and yet has no money—that is, money in the form of dollars. To keep growing, you convert dollars into other assets. In other words, you lock them up. But someday you're going to have to unlock them; and if you're not here, it may become a liquidation. The other word for liquidation is quite often—loss. You spend a lifetime accumulating assets. Someone will take them apart over night.

"If a person is willing to trade a lifetime for an estate, it should be worth keeping. It represents a life.

A long, long time ago, you got to the point where you were no longer working for bread and butter. Yesterday you earned enough money to buy two pairs of shoes, but you're only wearing one. Why only one? You could have purchased two sweaters, but you are only wearing one. So what are you doing? You're piling up something in the form of brick, stone, steel, land. This is your estate. This is your life. And, you know, you didn't build all this for the purpose of permitting it to fall apart. You prize your company. There are a lot of people depending on your company. I mean your family and the families of all the people you employ.

"Now let us put a floor beneath it. Sure, we can drain your company of cash. *Do you think the company could continue?* You're going to need some dollars, and I have guaranteed dollars. They're guaranteed and they're discounted. You never pay in the amount you get out. Furthermore, the gain is free of income tax. You're going to need some money. Why don't you use my dollars? They cost pennies apiece. Let me put the plan together and you take a look."

> *What are the price tags on your company continuity packages?*

They depend on the tax impact—the biggest factor that I know of in the entire field of life insurance. The tax impact creates the need for massive amounts of money. I have a case pending now for $15 million! Why? It isn't for the executive. It's to keep together what that person put together. It's to take care of tax impact on the estate.

"You'd like to be sure that your company goes on after you're no longer here. I'd like to show you that there is enough money to take care of your estate—without forcing the liquidation of estate assets."

Chapter 41

A Policy to Insure One Year's Profits

In close corporations—family held corporations—the owner usually wants his children to carry on. Sometimes when they do take over, because of inexperience, it's more of a threat to the company than the estate taxes. Is there any way you can insure the company's continuity in this case?

Yes, those who have the bulk of what they own wrapped up in their company quite often want the company to continue. Suppose they have a son and daughter. They want the children to carry on. And yet they know, the day they walk out, problems walk in. So tell a business owner:

"Here's a cushion, a cash cushion, for your children to lean on. They're bound to make some mistakes along the way. You know, there are two kinds of mistakes: Little ones and big ones. The little ones, the company can absorb. The big ones? They'll absorb the company. So, give your children something to lean on. Give them some time. Let's insure one year's profits. Give them a year's time to get their feet down solid and make the wheels go round."

What if your prospect tells you that he's going to deed his estate to his child? What would you tell him, Ben?

.I would say:

"Mr. Jones, the government levies a tax on your right to make money. They call it income tax, and you are familiar with it because you pay it every year. The government *also levies a tax on your right to transfer what is left to your family.* You are not familiar with it because you have never died. You cannot deed your entire estate to your child. You will deed it to the tax collector and your child. *And I promise you, the tax collector will come first and your child will come second.*

"Do you have lots of money? Is that money in your corporation? Now, what little you do have, your executors will have to take out and give the tax collector. You have difficulty running your company even *with* money. Do you think your child can run it *without* money?"

You see, you can have a beautiful case when you pinpoint the problem. He is proud of his company. He wants it to go on. He wants it to continue. No one wants to work a lifetime and then feel that everything he's built up is falling apart. He has a child and he wants the child to carry on. He would like the child to pick it up where Pop drops it and keep running with it. That's just human. That's normal. That's what we all want. But the tax structure won't let us do it. You *cannot* disregard the tax structure. If you do, you work for what? For nothing.

JOHN DOE
WHOLE LIFE ILLUSTRATION
Face Amount $ 750,000 Sex M Age 45
New York Life Insurance Co. Premiums Paid Annually
Rated Non-Smoker
LEDGER ILLUSTRATION

POLICY DIVIDEND OPTION Paid-Up Additions
DIVIDEND SURRENDER Premium only at age 50

YR	NET PREMIUM	POLICY CASH VALUE	DIVIDEND CASH VALUE	NET CASH VALUE	FACE AMOUNT OF ADDS	NET DEATH BENEFIT
1	20000	0	6202	6202	21527	771527
2	20000	0	15244	15244	42268	792268
3	20000	7500	26007	33507	70989	820989
4	20000	18000	38650	56650	103149	853149
5	20000	28500	53629	82129	138791	888791
6	0	39750	48971	88721	118820	868820
7	0	51750	44754	96504	101173	851173
8	0	63750	41064	104814	85881	835881
9	0	75750	38002	113752	72980	822980
10	0	88500	35694	124194	62531	812531
11	0	101250	34218	135468	54636	804636
12	0	116250	33657	152907	49251	799251
13	0	134250	34064	171689	46345	799345
14	0	152250	35530	191530	45809	799184
15	0	171000	38155	213467	47626	801376
16	0	189750	42067	236879	51797	806109
17	0	208500	47385	261510	58372	813434
18	0	227250	54294	287731	67378	823003
19	0	246750	62977	316477	78959	835146
20	0	265500	73647	346647	93247	849997

---- AGE --

65	0	282000	86525	376775	110409	867909
70	0	361500	190240	563740	242938	1004188
75	0	438750	385951	839701	468199	1233199
80	0	507000	717666	1239666	826023	1591023
99	0	750000	4845337	5610337	4552478	5317478

Policy Prem. of $ 14,025.00 w/ WP of $ 0.00 ADB of $ 0.00 PPO of $ 0.00

-------------- AVERAGE --------------------------------------- NET ------------------
Net Death Benefit 20th yr $ 822,480 Net Death Benefit 20th yr $ 849,997
Cost of a Dollar 20th yr $ .122 Cost of a Dollar 20th yr. $ .118

Dividends are not guaranteed. For explanation refer to form 11939.
This illustration was prepared for New York Life Insurance Co. using ISIS.
Insurance Sales Illustrations Systems is an independent computer software
service company and is not affiliated with any insurer or financial institution
Page # 1; ISIS Ver. 2.7 Date Prepared 04-25-1988 by BEN FELDMAN CLU

Chapter 42

How to Create a Guaranteed Market

*Suppose a prospect isn't interested in company con-
tinuity. Suppose he wants to sell in the event of his
death. What do you do then, Ben?*

I'll give you an example. I get a D&B on the XYZ
Company. I study the picture. The company's worth
about five million dollars. It looks like a one-man
operation. One man—he makes the wheels go round.
And that's a problem in itself—the problem of the
close corporation. And you know what that problem
is? The problem of a close corporation is that it's
closed: The money that he puts in is *closed in, locked
in*—locked into land and machinery, into bricks and
steel. A man spends his life putting money in—tell
me, how is he going to get that money *out?* Particularly after he's gone? Because the day he stops, the
company stops—and who wants the company then—at
any price? And if it *is* sold, it's sold only for what the

land and buildings and machinery will bring—and
that's only a fraction of what the man put in; it's not
the five million dollars or so the company is really
worth.

And what happens to this man's widow? He's going
to leave her *locked*-in to the company but *locked-out*
when it comes to cash. How is this man going to
unlock the value in the company—all the money he's
put into that company over the years? How is he going
to unlock that five million dollars so he can pass it on
to his widow? You know, the widow is much better
off with five million dollars in U.S. bonds than five
million dollars in bricks and machinery.

So this man has a problem—a five-million–dollar
problem.

The moment he walks out, he wants his widow
bailed out. He wants to sell the company after he dies.
But how can he be sure there's going to be a buyer?
After all, it's a close corporation. *He's* the company.
When he's gone, what's the company worth? And if
there is a buyer, how can the man be sure the buyer
will pay the price tag that this man puts on the company? And you can be sure that the price tag will be a
big one. So when you look through this man's eyes,
you see that this problem is a big one—a problem that
might look to him like it could never be solved.

But why can't you *guarantee a market* for his company? It's simply an agreement worked out between
two companies. When that keyperson dies, the other
company buys. And you guarantee the money with
life insurance on the keyperson's life. The company
that buys is the beneficiary.

And don't forget, the company president who *buys*
pays for the acquired company with *discounted* dol-

lars. Look what a wonderful thing life insurance is: The *buyer* pays pennies on the dollar. And yet the *seller* gets every dollar written on the price tag! You can say:

"Everybody will know that your widow will have to pay the tax, so it won't be possible for her to get a good price on anything that has to be sold. Let me show you how to protect your widow against bargain seekers. I will create a guaranteed market—a policy designed to convert bricks and steel into dollars, so your family will end up with dollars instead of frozen assets."

Ben, you looked at the problem through the eyes of the man who wanted to sell. How about looking at it through the eyes of the person you'll have to convince to do the buying. Remember, it's that person who'll be paying the premiums. Just how would I go about convincing her or him?

Ask yourself: What's this executive's problem? *My competitor's put a five-hundred-thousand-dollar price tag on his company. But that's too much for me. How can I buy it for less?* You say to the potential buyer, "How would you like to buy your competitor's company for pennies on the dollar?" Would he? You bet your life he would.

But don't stop there. Remember, this businessperson is watching pennies. Say:

"From a $20,000 premium, an average of $20,000 is plowed back into cash value. And, somewhere down the road, we guarantee to pay at least $1 million. How many years would it take you to pay in the amount we pay out?"

It's a very simple package designed to create cash to buy a competitive business—a "purchase package."

Chapter 43

How to Guarantee Stock Redemption

Suppose the owner doesn't want to sell the company but just wants to be sure that the company has the money to redeem his stock when he walks out. What can you do about that, Ben?

Let's take a specific instance. I have a case. It's a large trucking company. Going over the D&B, I see it's a typical family company—father, son, and son-in-law. I find the party who started the company is getting on in years and is probably no longer active. I can see a need for insurance to pay estate taxes to keep together what they've put together. I can also see a need for cash to redeem stock.

Visualize what happens when the father dies. The family doesn't want outsiders to buy the stock. They want the stock redeemed so that it can remain closely held. The family would be willing to redeem the stock if they had the money. But something has to be done to pay the tax.

The problem here is this: The corporation must have insurance on the father to redeem his stock. They need estate dollars. The widow will be better off with cash than she will with shares of stock from which she can get little or no income. We need insurance on the boys to redeem the stock. The family will be better off with the cash.

The stock's got a basic value of two million dollars. The father owns 40 percent and the rest is broken up among the children—12 percent, 12 percent, 12 percent, 12 percent, and 12 percent. Now, if the stock of the father is redeemed, then the equity of the children remains equal. The father intended it to be equal or he wouldn't have given them equal amounts. Let's keep it that way.

Let's not have the mother dependent on what may happen once her husband's gone; make her independent. See that there's enough cash to bail out the estate, enough cash to redeem the father's stock. Let her have her independence. Let the children go on and do with the company what they are capable of doing.

This is one of my cold prospects. I haven't made the call yet. Look how much time you spend getting ready to get ready. You finally get to the point where you know as much about the company as the prospect knows. When you make the call, you can hit home quickly, simply; you can show the tax impact.

Don't most companies already have corporate insurance to guarantee stock redemption?

You'll find very few companies that have corporate insurance. And any insurance they have, they bought years ago; it's outmoded. Companies grow and continue to grow. So you can find a need for more insurance. You underwrite the problems of today, then go a little farther and underwrite tomorrow—because the company will get bigger. Say to the prospect:

"Have you thought about a public offering of your stock? What about a private offering? It's much simpler, and it will also get your dollars out. It's simply an agreement between you and your company, with my company furnishing the money."

Ben, you've been talking about close corporations. How shall I approach the problem of stock redemption in a public corporation?

The key to insurance in a public corporation is this: A substantial stockholder still needs estate tax dollars. In all probability, her stock will need to be sold. Set up a guaranteed market for her stock through the company, and your company will guarantee the cash. Say to the woman:

"You will have the certainty of a guaranteed market with guaranteed dollars—plus, your company gets your stock at a discount."

Chapter 44

Partnership: See-Saw Insurance

You've shown me many ways to use insurance to keep a close corporation going after the owner's death—and also help the family. Do you have a package that applies to partnerships—can you tell me how that works?

Did you ever hear of see-saw insurance? It's a very simple expression for what some people call business insurance. There are two men (or women) in business, and they're on a see-saw. They balance each other.

But, can you imagine one see-sawing if the other gets off? If one gets off, the other falls off. One can't see-saw alone.

Here again, I'll walk in and say: "Look, put me on your payroll for $50 a day or $50 a week or whatever. And the day your partner falls off, I'll bring you enough money to buy out his business interest."

Why does he want to buy out his partner's interest? You know, when a partner walks out, his widow walks in. What does she know about the business? The surviving partner might not want to conduct his business with his partner's widow. If the business is to continue, the surviving partner will want to buy out the widow.

But has he got the cash? His business is like any other business—it's stones and steel—it's *not* liquid assets. He just can't liquidate half the business without destroying the whole business. If you and I had a partnership worth two hundred thousand dollars, and we owned it equally, and one of us dies—do you think the other one of us could just cut the company in half and pull out the hundred thousand? *You could not. I could not.* So there's a problem: *How is a partner to get the cash to buy out the other partner's survivor without destroying the company?*

Life insurance can easily solve that problem. It's simple. The partners insure each other. Each is the other's beneficiary. And there's an agreement to use the money to buy out the deceased partner's spouse. So everybody's happy—the remaining partner *and* the spouse. Tell me, isn't the survivor much better off with money that's no longer exposed to risk? Isn't she or he better off to have the money? Say to a partner:

"You know, a partnership is like a see-saw: When one partner gets off, the other partner falls off. Here's a plan to buy out your partner—for pennies on the dollar. When one dies, the other buys. Let me show it to you."

Don't you find many partnerships already have agreements to buy each other out in the event of one partner's death?

Yes. It's an agreement that if you die, I buy. All your interest is offered for sale. I have first right to buy. But I better have the money. I've seen binding agreements: If you die, I must buy. Yet I won't have the money. What good is the agreement? It's an obligation. I've got to buy. But I don't have the money. Maybe I can borrow it. Maybe I can't. Say to a partner:

"This is a plan designed to create cash for your partner's half of the business. You set aside $500 a month. If nothing happens, we will give you back your money. If something happens, we will give you back your money and his share besides. Let me put it together. . . ."

Suppose one of the partners is appreciably older;
how do you handle the situation?

In case of a cross-purchase with the younger partner paying a higher premium for the older partner, say to the younger partner, "You pay more, but we pay sooner."

Chapter 45

One Policy for the Tax Collector, Another Policy for Your Family

*You've been telling me, Ben, how insurance can help
a company from falling apart. But what about the
widow and the children? What can I do about the
man's family?*

The man's family needs to go on living. Is there a
source of income? A life insurance contract has options that are *designed* to provide an income. You
need to make sure that there will be a livable lifetime
income for the family.

For example: The man's been earning $5,000 a
month. The family can live on $3,750 a month. Add
an extra $1,000 in reserve in case the widow needs
extra money for emergencies, for opportunities, for gifts
to grandchildren—whatever she needs it for. If she
doesn't use the extra money, there'll be cash to absorb
the cash impact on *her* estate.

In handling a close corporation case, in the beginning what you do is the emergency work—what you

do is to create the cash for what has to be paid. You know what has to be paid? The day I walk out creditors walk in. You know who they are? My banker walks in. I made a promise to pay him some money. He wants some money. The IRS walks in. These debts must come first. But along with showing a prospect how these debts can be paid, tell him: "Here's an income for your family."

Explain to the prospect: "Your widow has no right to expect your company to pay her an income. Is she performing a service? What service? Can she step into your shoes and do what you've been doing? Will she be eligible to take out salary the way you've been taking it out? No. She owns pieces of paper. They pay no dividend. What will she do with them?"

Tell the prospect that there should be an income and a personal policy—even a split dollar policy—with the corporation paying the bulk of the premium. "There is a plan by which the corporation pays the premium. You have a very minor cost. Yet, the bulk of the proceeds ultimately go to your family."

Say, "One policy for the tax collector, and one policy for your family."

Of course, you can also give him a policy for his banker, and so on.

Chapter 46

The Salary Continuation Package

Can't you also use options, Ben, to protect the widow?

Yes, you can build packages out of options.

"Mr. Jones, how would you like your widow to have five thousand dollars a month for life?"

By taking advantage of an option, you can arrange that five thousand dollars a month—that's the man's salary. So you can show the prospect that you have an idea how his widow can continue to receive his salary even after he's gone.

What do I call this package? It's my *salary continuation package*.

Chapter 47

A Package to Insure Company Credit

Ben, a prospect might say, "I need a large sum of money to keep my company going while I'm alive so my company can progress, move ahead. But how can I guarantee the bank that my company will be able to pay it back in case something happens to me?"

You should insure your company's credit. It will tend to guarantee continuity for your name. Everyone who runs a closely held business has this kind of problem. A bank won't let a keyperson's company borrow money unless the keyperson promises to pay it back—because, after all, *she's* the company. But how can she keep her promise if she runs out of time? Where's the money to come from?

When a woman borrows, it's because she needs it. If she needs it, she spends it. She doesn't have any money. And if she runs out of time, how's the bank going to get its money back? You know something? The bank is not going to let her have the money unless the bank is sure she can keep her promise.

JOHN DOE
WHOLE LIFE ILLUSTRATION AD87
Face Amount $ 1,000,000 Sex M Age 45
New York Life Insurance Co.   Premiums Paid Annually
Rated Standard Non-Smoker
POP WITH NET DEATH BENEFIT EOY

POLICY DIVIDEND OPTION Paid-Up Additions
DIVIDEND SURRENDER Premium only at age 55

YR	NET PREMIUM P.O.Y.	POLICY CASH VALUE P.O.Y.	CASH VALUE OF PAID-UP ADDITIONS E.O.Y.	NET CASH VALUE F.O.Y.	FACE AMOUNT OF ADDITIONS E.O.Y.	NET DEATH BENEFIT E.O.Y.
1	18,690	0	0	0	0	1,000,000
2	18,690	0	2,500	2,500	8,364	1,008,364
3	18,690	10,000	6,364	16,364	20,526	1,020,526
4	18,690	24,000	11,724	35,724	36,462	1,036,462
5	18,690	38,000	18,827	56,827	56,483	1,056,483
6	18,690	53,000	27,841	80,841	80,604	1,080,604
7	18,690	69,000	39,008	108,008	109,018	1,109,018
8	18,690	85,000	52,588	137,588	141,939	1,141,939
9	18,690	101,000	68,877	169,877	179,629	1,179,629
10	18,690	118,000	88,220	206,220	222,434	1,222,434
11	0	135,000	90,341	225,341	175,311	1,175,311
12	0	155,000	94,074	253,074	174,759	1,174,759
13	0	179,000	99,520	283,020	177,956	1,181,956
14	0	203,000	106,837	314,837	184,775	1,189,275
15	0	228,000	116,196	349,946	195,214	1,200,214
16	0	253,000	127,810	387,560	209,303	1,215,053
17	0	278,000	141,876	427,376	227,144	1,233,894
18	0	303,000	158,694	469,944	248,800	1,256,300
19	0	329,000	178,552	516,552	274,518	1,282,768
20	0	354,000	201,798	565,798	304,516	1,313,516
***** AGE *****						
65	0	376,000	228,778	615,778	339,083	1,349,083
70	0	482,000	430,245	928,245	586,897	1,601,897
75	0	585,000	786,218	1,391,218	985,769	2,005,769
80	0	676,000	1,369,496	2,065,496	1,603,814	2,623,814
99	0	1,000,000	8,428,173	9,448,173	7,941,943	8,961,943

Policy Prem of $18,690.00 w/ WP of $ 0.00 ADB of $ 0.00 PPO of $ 0.00

************** AVERAGE **************   ************** NET **************
Net Death Benefit 20th yr $ 1,142,804 Net Death Benefit 20th yr $ 1,313,516
Cost of a Dollar 20th yr $ 0.164 Cost of a Dollar 20th yr $ 0.142

This illustration was prepared using I.S.I.S. 705 S. Wells Ave., Reno, NV 89502
which is an independent Computer Software Service Company and is not affiliated
with any Insurer or Financial Institution.
Page # 1; Date Prepared 04-27-1988

Now life insurance can solve that problem. Life insurance puts a floor under time. Say to a prospect:

"Sooner or later you're going to need more money from the bank. Your company is growing; you're going to need more cash to keep it growing. But will the bank give you the credit line you need unless you can guarantee the money in case something happens to you? Here's an idea: *A special contract* that insures corporate credit. Let me show it to you. . . ."

Here's an illustration on a man, aged 45, for one million dollars (page 142).

Why does this man need a million dollars? He needs it because he's a one-man corporation and he's growing and he needs money with which to grow. So he goes to banks to ask for money, and the banks want to know:

"If we lend you this money, are you going to pay it back? We have confidence that you'll pay it back—as long as you're here. But what happens if you wrap your car around a tree? We don't want to run your company. We're in the banking business. We don't want your company. We want the million dollars."

So I say to my prospect:

"With the stroke of a pen, I can create that million dollars for you. The day you walk out, a million dollars walks in.

"Look at the illustration. If you should die ten years from now, your corporation will have put $186,900 in this policy. You know what my company will do?

"We'll give you back the total cash value—which is $206,000—a complete recovery of cost—and, in addition, I'll come in personally and bring a check for one million dollars, tax-free.

"Now, tell me—where else can you get a million dollars with no cost at all?"

It's a simple illustration, but it's graphic, exciting, effective.

Chapter 48

How to Work Along with the Banks to Increase Your Volume

Do you ever help a prospect get a loan by working along with a bank and setting up the insurance?

If you present a good idea to a bank, it will loan you the money. But the bank can't guarantee the time. When a bank makes a loan to the borrower, it's really making a loan based on confidence in what he's going to do with the money. The bank knows he's going to spend the money. The money will lose its identity; it'll become brick, stone, steel—everything except dollars.

Now if the borrower has enough time, he'll make his plan work out. He'll keep his commitments, and he'll repay the loan. But if the borrower walks out, the bank doesn't want to be in a position of liquidating his company. The bank wants to be sure to get its money back. That's where I can work along with my client and the bank.

I have a case: He's got a million dollars in insurance. He doesn't need anymore. He doesn't want any more. He called me. He said, "I have a chance to buy a new company. I need $750,000. Where can I get that much money? You've been telling me about a bank in Youngstown that might be receptive. The new plant will be in Youngstown."

I set up an appointment between the banker and myself and this party. He needs money, and the bank is looking for a new customer—and if the deal looks good to them, they'll make the loan. If they make the loan, he needs time to pay it back. So I write $750,000 to cover it.

You know something? When you write any policy payable to a company, you tend to make the company worth a little more money. Now, if you and I owned the ABC company equally, and if I died—somehow, someone would have to come up with enough money to pay for my stock. Say, the bank had loaned the company $750,000, and the life insurance policy paid it back. Suddenly, the company is worth $750,000 more. Now my stock is worth $375,000 more. We'll need some more insurance. It grows and it grows. It never stops.

Does a bank ever pay premiums on the policy?

Should there be a keyperson policy assigned to the bank, quite often the bank will advance the money to pay the premiums for the policy as part of the loan. This is a very small price to pay for insuring the loan.

Keep in mind that, other than the first premium, the bulk of everything paid in simply piles up—

becomes cash value. Show your banks how a contract creates cash. Show them that there's usually a tremendous gain to the corporation, and there's no income tax. It's a tax-free addition to corporate surplus.

Cultivate your banks. It's a new frontier of creative selling.

Chapter 49

How to Sell Keyperson Insurance

How about keyperson insurance—doesn't that create company credit?

Keypeople create corporate credit. Sometimes corporations find themselves locked up and locked out. This happens when a keyperson dies, unless he's insured.

What's your approach when talking to a keyperson?

Ask her, "Did you ever take a vacation? Ever go away for a couple of weeks?"

She'll say, "Yes."

"Any problems?"

She'll say, "No."

148

"Could you take a month off?"

"Yes."

"Could you take a year off?"

Maybe she'll hesitate a little while. Maybe there'd be some problems if she took a year off.

Then tell her:

"You know, Ms. Jones, no woman has a lease on life. One of these days you're going to walk out the door and you're *never* coming back. You think that would have a bearing on corporate credit? Corporate credit is very important to the continuity of your company and all the people depending on it, including your family. There's the telephone. Why don't you call your banker. Call your banker and ask this question: 'If I walk out and will never come back, and a short time later the tax collector walks in and takes all the money, will it have any bearing on my company's credit line? Or will the bank be willing to go along as they have in the past?' "

I have never yet found a woman brave enough to make that call.

Say to that woman, "Do you think your bank will extend the same credit line to one who takes your place?"

What's your approach when you're talking to the head of a company about other keypeople?

"Mr. Jones, your accountant even puts a box of stationery on your balance sheet but ignores the person who makes your company a million dollars. While no one is indispensable, nor is your equipment or your building, yet you insure the equipment and building because you can't get a loan without insuring them.

"Yet machines and buildings don't make money. Only management—keypeople—make money. When you lose a keyperson you lose money. With him or her gone, it would simply be money at work. The contrast would be tremendous.

"Compare the earnings on money with the earnings of a keyperson. One hundred thousand dollars may earn $8,000 a year. The same amount wrapped up in a company operated by a keyperson may earn $20,000 to $50,000. The value of a keyperson is many times the value of money.

"The ability of keypeople means the difference between profit and loss. Insuring them means insuring profits. The keypeople are worth what you insure them for, and they should be insured for what they are worth. My company offers a policy that costs three cents per dollar but returns the dollar plus the three cents.

"I'm not saying that a person is indispensable. I'm only saying that the loss of a keyperson can create problems.

"You've got a good many men and women working for you. Why don't you hire one more? Me. Put me on your payroll. Sixty dollars a day. Set up a special account for me and put $60 a day in it, and I'll set up a special account for you and put $1 million in it! You know, in seven or eight years the dividend account will be great enough to pay the premiums on the policy for the rest of the keyperson's life. You'll never be able to put in what you're someday going to take out. Suppose I put it together and you take a look?"

When you sell keyperson insurance, do you look down the road?

You plan on living, don't you? No one plans on dying. Not today. Maybe tomorrow, but not today. So when I prepare my illustrations, I look down the road because tomorrow is coming.

"And, Ms. Jones, if you don't want to go all the way with a permanent block of insurance today, take an option—buy a term policy—insure your insurability— at least do that. And when the time comes, look, and exercise your option."

Chapter 50

The Bonus Policy

I had this keyperson case. I walked into this closely-held family company and found a man in his fifties who had been running pretty hard. The company represented the bulk of everything he owned in the world. It was growing and expanding. He was very proud of it. He wanted the company and the company name to be carried on by his son. His son was still a boy, not yet mature enough to step into his father's shoes. But the father had built a management team; and this team, if it could be locked in, could carry the company until the boy was mature enough to take over.

I said to this man:

"The biggest assets you have are these key people, and yet how can you be sure—if you get on the wrong

152

airplane or in the wrong car, and one day you are
gone—how can you be sure that these men and women
will continue carrying your company on for the benefit of your family? Don't you think you should try to
lock them in, or tie them up, in some manner? Don't
you think you should give them a little something
more so they'll be a little more likely to stay instead of
walking away?

"Your corporation can pay for this insurance. We
have a special plan for special people. We call it a
split dollar policy. It's an arrangement whereby these
men and women receive benefits over and above the
salary they're receiving now. Tell a keyperson: 'Look,
Joe, if something happens to you, I'm going to pay off
the mortgage on your home, and I'm going to educate
your children. This is all free. It won't cost you a
penny."

The I say to the corporate head: "Over and above
what it will do for the keypersons, let me tell you
what it will do for you. It will pay your company
$500,000 to indemnify for the loss of a keyperson. It'll
return to your company all premiums you've paid.
Suppose I put it together and you take a look?"

I call it the *Bonus Policy*. It's simply a block of
whole life.

What was the size of the policy?

In this case, I wrote two policies, each for $500,000.
The keypeople are tickled to death. The man who
owns the company is very happy.

JOHN DOE
WHOLE LIFE ILLUSTRATION
Face Amount $ 750,000 Sex M Age 50
New York Life Insurance Co. Premiums Paid Annually
Rated Non-Smoker
SPLIT DOLLAR LEDGER ILLUSTRATION

POLICY DIVIDEND OPTION Paid-Up Additions
DIVIDEND SURRENDER Premium only at age 65
SPLIT DOLLAR TYPE Reverse ER's Face Amt in 1000's fixed at 500
ECONOMIC BENEFIT RATES for Rev Split Dol are P.S. 58 ending at EE's age 65

YR	AGE	EMPLOYER PREMIUM	EMPLOYEE PREMIUM	EMPLOYER CASH VALUE	EMPLOYEE CASH VALUE	EMPLOYERS NET DEATH BENEFIT	EMPLOYEE NET DEATH BENEFIT
1	50	4610	13427	0	0	500000	250000
2	51	4985	13052	0	2318	500000	250000
3	52	5395	12642	0	16475	500000	256478
4	53	5845	12192	0	35151	500000	266128
5	54	6335	11702	0	55610	500000	279082
6	55	6870	11167	0	78002	500000	295663
7	56	7455	10582	0	103246	500000	315858
8	57	8090	9947	0	131512	500000	339696
9	58	8780	9257	0	162257	500000	367184
10	59	9540	8497	0	199440	500000	398396
11	60	10365	7672	0	237509	500000	437153
12	61	11265	6772	0	278988	500000	477250
13	62	12250	5787	0	329481	500000	521829
14	63	13315	4722	0	384096	500000	571158
15	64	14490	3547	0	443259	500000	625524
16	65	0	0	0	487630	0	1151884
17	66	0	0	0	535510	0	1182695
18	67	0	0	0	587147	0	1218042
19	68	0	0	0	642749	0	1257989
20	69	0	0	0	702631	0	1302520
-- AGE							
65	65	0	0	0	487630	0	1151884
70	70	0	0	0	763916	0	1351806
75	75	0	0	0	1148271	0	1679182
80	80	0	0	0	1709856	0	2188148
99	99	0	0	0	7814189	0	7412773

Policy Prem. of $ 18,037.50 w/ WP of $ 0.00 ADB of $ 0.00 PPO of $ 0.0
--------------- AVERAGE ------------------------------- NET ----------------
Net Death Benefit 20th yr $ 963,226 Net Death Benefit 20th yr $ 1,302,520
Cost of a Dollar 20th yr $ .281   Cost of a Dollar 20th yr. $ .208

Page # 1; ISIS Ver. 2.7 Date Prepared 04-25-1988 by BEN FELDMAN CLU

Chapter 51

How to Create a Sale by Switching to a Younger Keyperson

Ben, a lot of us have cases where we insure a keyperson to back up a corporate credit line, and the insurance is assigned to a bank. As the years go by, the keyperson grows older, and a young man or woman in the company becomes the real keyperson and takes over the drive of the company. What do you do about it?

I had such a case.

I went up to the older man and I said, "You know, this young woman seems to have become very active in your company. I imagine she could pretty much run it now, couldn't she?"

The older man said, "Certainly she could. I just sort of keep my finger on it now, but Susan is really running it. I think she could almost run it on her own."

I said, "You know, Ray, we locked up a big chunk of your corporate insurance when we assigned it to the bank. If we could persuade the bank that continuity for the company is built around Susan—ask the bank to let us substitute some insurance on her and release some of the coverage on you—it might be well worthwhile."

That's exactly what we did. I approached the bank. I told the bankers that the young woman, not the old man, was the keyperson. Wouldn't they be better off having substantial insurance on the new keyperson and releasing some of the insurance on the older man? They said they'd be willing to do this.

The man who owned the company was tickled to death to get his insurance back. We released the insurance on the older man and substituted insurance on the younger keyperson.

Chapter 52

A Special Contract for the Prospect Who Has too Much Money

How can anyone have too much money, Ben?

A man or woman runs, runs, and runs, and after a while he has his business on a pretty good basis, with all the working capital he needs. He begins to pile up dollars—the kind of dollars he needs for inventory or for a new addition to the building—surplus dollars. Sections 531-537 of the Internal Revenue Code are designed to prevent what Uncle Sam calls unreasonable accumulation of surplus. What is unreasonable? "The surplus money is needed to run the business," the man argues. Well, prove it! The money's not wrapped up in the business. He's not using it. It's cash in a checkbook—in a certificate of deposit or in commercial paper. It's not in the business. It's surplus.

The government states that for non-service-oriented corporations, you're allowed to accumulate up to $250,000. When you go over that, red flags go up. The IRS takes a look and says: "Mr. Jones, you can't do this. But you did do it. So there's an extra tax. The tax, instead of being 34 percent is going to be 61 percent. It can go up as high as 72 percent. You made it, but you can't keep it."

It's called unreasonable accumulation—too much money. The money isn't the person's who earned it. It belongs to Uncle Sam. And Uncle Sam's going to take it. Not only is he going to take it. But he's going to penalize the person for not giving it to him sooner.

Is there a legal way by which a person can avoid this tremendous tax impact?

The man or woman in business makes business decisions every day, and many of the decisions represent security for the company, continuity for the company. Most people look down the road and realize that no one has a lease on life. "Some day something will happen to me." Say to this prospect:

You know, there's another section of the Internal Revenue Code, section 303, that's designed to really help people like you. The bulk of your estate is not in your pocket; it's in the company. The government realizes that it's not possible to get money out of that corporation without creating a big hole. But the government wants its money. The tax impact on the estate is creating your problem. A good corporate decision on your part is to make sure that the money the government will some day ask your family for will be available without the liquidation of assets.

"You know, when I find out your company has to be sold under forced liquidation, I'm going to be buying it. You know why? Because I'm not going to pay for it. I'm going to 'steal' it. I'm going to get it for nothing, or as close to nothing as possible. That's what you would do with my company. So a good decision on your part would be to do what has to be done.

"Therefore, there should be a big, big bulk of keyperson coverage on you—money that walks in when you walk out. The coverage is not designed to make anybody money; it's just designed to keep together what you've put together. It's a good decision to buy those dollars for pennies apiece. If you're insurable, my company will put into escrow the million dollars that the government might ask for. If you don't let my company do it, then your family will have to do it. Let me put it together. . . ."

What I'm saying is that this person has too much money and must invest it as outlined in keyperson insurance. That would not be considered unreasonable or the government wouldn't have designed a code that permits stock redemption; the government knows there has to be money with which to redeem the stock. So, the government designed 531-537 to prevent too much money, and it designed 303 to permit stock redemptions.

The contract I've outlined will accumulate a lot of money. But wouldn't it be difficult to say it was an unreasonable accumulation? In all the years that have gone by, there have been many companies that have had a 531-537 problem, but to my knowlege there's yet to be a case where life insurance was involved that went to litigation.

Chapter 53

Use It or Lose It: That's the Way It Works with the Federal Gift Tax Exclusion

While we're on the subject of tax impact, can you tell me how you use gifts to help a prospect lessen that impact?

Use it or lose it. When you have the background on the statement—use it or lose it—you'll understand. Use *what*? Lose *what*?

Use it. The government levies a tax on your ability to make money. They call it income tax. The government levies a tax on your right to transfer what's left to your family. They call that estate tax. But the government also gives you a right—the right to make transfers of money free of tax. The government calls this your gift tax exemption. You can make a gift to any one person each year of up to $10,000. Any time during the year—but *only* during the year.

Or lose it. Gift tax exemptions lapse each year on December 31st. Either you use them or lose them. It costs you nothing to use them. It costs you a lot if you don't. The gift exemption—use it or lose it!

The gift tax exemption renews the following year. But if you didn't use it for last year, you lost it. What does it cost to lose it? Let's see:

You'd like to make a gift of $10,000. To whom? Let's say to your daughter. And under the terms of your will it will be subject to estate tax. Using the right to make the gift *now*, you give her $10,000 on which you pay no tax. And $10,000 out of your estate may save three thousand dollars. You can save more than you can earn. Where can you put a dollar that will earn 30 percent? I know where you can put a dollar where it will *save* 30 percent. Because the tax on the top dollar in the estate will be 30 percent.

Will you show me how you use the federal gift tax exclusion to sell insurance?

I had this case years ago when the gift tax exemption was limited to $3,000 per person per year.

Here was a man past 80 years of age and totally blind. He had been on disability income with New York Life and Prudential for about 30 years. The man had a family. This man had a great deal of courage and a real good mind. He had succeeded with the help of his children in building a successful business, a very substantial estate.

What man wants to run all his life piling up assets and then someday have a large part of those assets go down the drain? In this case, the man had no wife, no marital deduction. That meant Uncle Sam would take an even larger share of the estate.

YOUR GRANDSON
WHOLE LIFE ILLUSTRATION
Face Amount $ 500,000 Sex M Age 15
New York Life Insurance Co. Premiums Paid Annually
Rated Standard
LEDGER ILLUSTRATION

POLICY DIVIDEND OPTION Paid-Up Additions
DIVIDEND SURRENDER Premium only at age 25

YR	NET PREMIUM	POLICY CASH VALUE	DIVIDEND CASH VALUE	NET CASH VALUE	FACE AMOUNT OF ADDS	NET DEATH BENEFIT
1	10000	0	7016	7016	74840	574840
2	10000	0	15908	15908	147061	647061
3	10000	0	25806	25806	233717	733717
4	10000	0	36794	36794	324655	824655
5	10000	0	49204	49204	420054	920054
6	10000	2000	62997	64997	522192	1022192
7	10000	4500	78313	82813	629608	1129608
8	10000	6500	95316	101816	742369	1242369
9	10000	9000	114186	123186	860538	1360538
10	10000	11500	135127	146627	984266	1484266
11	0	14500	147388	161888	1035298	1535298
12	0	18500	161120	179620	1090536	1590536
13	0	22000	176508	198508	1150299	1650299
14	0	26000	193737	219737	1214963	1714963
15	0	30000	213019	243019	1284952	1784952
16	0	34000	234608	268608	1360676	1860676
17	0	38500	258785	297285	1442596	1942596
18	0	43000	285810	328810	1531278	2031278
19	0	47500	316022	363522	1627015	2127015
20	0	52500	349730	404230	1730523	2230523
---- AGE						
65	0	255000	7571230	7829980	12780840	13284590
70	0	296500	11879330	12179580	17651980	18155730
75	0	337000	18362710	18703460	24409200	24912950
80	0	372500	28015110	28391360	34084088	34587840
98	0	487000	123160 K	123651 K	118577 K	119081 K

Policy Prem. of $ 3,230.00 w/ WP of $ 0.00 ADB of $ 0.00 PPO of $ 0.00
--------------- AVERAGE ----------------------------------- NET ----------------
Net Death Benefit 20th yr $ 1,420,372 Net Death Benefit 20th yr $ 2,230,523
Cost of a Dollar 20th yr $ .07 Cost of a Dollar 20th yr. $ .045

It wasn't hard to show this man that it was late—almost too late—and that he should begin thinking about conserving the dollars for which he had exchanged a lifetime.

Certainly, that man was not insurable. What could he do?

Among the children and grandchildren there were ten beneficiaries. I set up ten policies, each with an exact $3,000 annual premium. He paid $30,000 in December and he paid $30,000 in January. He went on to get those policies paid up very quickly. I wrote ten policies, ranging between $30,000 and $40,000. Uncle Sam will subsidize a major part of the premiums through tax savings on the estate of the old man.

Year by year, the children and grandchildren were getting their share of the estate. What a wonderful gift for the children! They'll never forget who gave it to them.

Now, there are other men, and women like that—people with the same problem. I have a package for those people. It's called *Dollars for Your Grandchildren*.

What grandparents don't want to help their grandchildren? My *Grandchildren Package*—what's it for? To see to it that the children and grandchildren get their fair share of the estate.

Say to a prospect:

"Let's reduce the estate by making gifts to the people who are going to get it anyway—your grandchildren. Do it my way, without tax. It can be done as a gift to the grandchildren with your daughter as custodian. This means you still have effective control through her. The tax savings will pay for most of their education. Additionally, down the road when your

YOUR GRANDSON
WHOLE LIFE ILLUSTRATION
Face Amount $ 500,000 Sex M Age 15
New York Life Insurance Co.   Premiums Paid Annually
Rated Standard
LEDGER ILLUSTRATION

POLICY DIVIDEND OPTION Paid-Up Additions
DIVIDEND SURRENDER Surrender table

YR	NET PREMIUM	POLICY CASH VALUE	DIVIDEND CASH VALUE	NET CASH VALUE	FACE AMOUNT OF ADDS	NET DEATH BENEFIT
1	10000	0	7016	7016	74840	574840
2	10000	0	15908	15908	147061	647061
3	10000	0	25806	25806	233717	733717
4	10000	0	36794	36794	324655	824655
5	10000	0	49204	49204	420054	920054
6	10000	2000	62997	64997	522192	1022192
7	10000	4500	78313	82813	629608	1129608
8	10000	6500	95316	101816	742369	1242369
9	10000	9000	114186	123186	860538	1360538
10	10000	11500	135127	146627	984266	1484266
11	0	14500	147388	161888	1035298	1535298
12	0	18500	161120	179620	1090536	1590536
13	0	22000	176508	198508	1150299	1650299
14	0	26000	193737	219737	1214963	1714963
15	0	30000	213019	243019	1284952	1784952
16	-20000	34000	212511	246511	1230957	1730957
17	-20000	38500	212263	250763	1180130	1680130
18	-20000	43000	212284	255284	1132680	1632680
19	-20000	47500	212631	260131	1088519	1588519
20	-20000	52500	213314	267814	1047862	1547862
---- AGE						
65	-20000	255000	786816	1045566	1303043	1806793
70	-20000	296500	1181997	1482247	1730475	2234225
75	-20000	337000	1792157	2132907	2354824	2858574
80	-20000	372500	2717788	3094038	3278405	3782155
98	-20000	487000	12023270	12514020	11542110	12045860

Policy Prem. of $ 3,230.00 w/ WP of $ 0.00 ADB of $ 0.00 PPO of $ 0.00
---------------- AVERAGE -- NET ----------------
Net Death Benefit 20th yr $ 1,319,775   Net Death Benefit 20th yr $ 1,547,862
Cost of a Dollar 20th yr $ .076   Cost of a Dollar 20th yr. $ .065

Dividends are not guaranteed. For explanation refer to form 11939.
This illustration was prepared for New York Life Insurance Co. using ISIS.
Insurance Sales Illustrations Systems is an independent computer software
service company and is not affiliated with any insurer or financial institution.
Page # 1; ISIS Ver. 2.7 Date Prepared 04-11-1988 by BEN FELDMAN CLU

grandchildren are 25 or 35, the cash value in the policy will have grown to such an extent that annual withdrawals can be made to provide them with annual income that can continue indefinitely—a little something extra from their grandparents."

Ben, what would you say is the key to such cases?

The key to such cases? Simply keeping what you've got. Why spend a lifetime putting it together and then let it go down the drain?

Remember: There's a price tag on everything—doing something and doing nothing. And, quite often, the price tag on doing nothing is much bigger than the price tag on doing something.

Chapter 54

How to Have Charitable Contributions Go on Forever— Painlessly

Many companies make charitable contributions as part of their tax program. Certainly, these programs would be in jeopardy with the death of a keyperson in a closely-held corporation. Do you run into this kind of problem. And, if so, how do you solve it?

As you make your calls, from time to time you find companies that are very, very charitable. These companies have been systematically and consistently making substantial gifts to charitable institutions in the community. These gifts are often given with such regularity that they become a part of the charitable institution's budget. The institution depends upon them.

    I ran into a closely-held family company. It was started by the father, now deceased. It was carried on by a very able mother, also now deceased. It is being carried on by the children. One of the children is the keyperson of the corporation.

The children had been given their own foundation, established in honor of their parents. The children had been giving the maximum corporate 5 percent to the foundation. The foundation had been distributing every penny of this money to charitable institutions in the community. These institutions had reached the point where they counted on this money. It was almost a must in their budgets. In addition, the children were giving their maximum personal contributions to other charitable institutions.

I pointed out to the children:

"You know, what you're doing is wonderful. But you have set a precedent. These institutions depend on this money coming from you and your company. What will happen somewhere down the road if something happens to your keyperson? It may be quite a load for you to keep on doing what you are doing, and it may be awkward to discontinue what you are doing. I have an idea. It can be very, very realistic. Let's see if we can put it together...."

I wrote a $500,000 policy on the life of the keyperson the policy to be paid by the corporation. The proceeds of the policy were broken into two parts: One part, equal to the cash value, was to be retained by the corporation; the other part, equal to the face value, was to flow into their non-profit foundation.

The total premium was only $20,000 a year—most of which was retained through cash value. There is no load on the corporation once the policy becomes a claim.

Someday $500,000, the face amount of the policy, will flow into the foundation. The $500,000, invested at only 8 percent will earn $40,000 a year forever. Insurance creates enough capital to make the charitable contributions painless and permanent.

Chapter 55

How to Buy a
Big Contract

*Ben, you've been talking about big policies. Do you
have trouble getting the underwriting?*

Ironic as it may sound, a big contract is harder to buy
than it is to sell. Many years, ago it was hard to buy
$100,000. You could buy $10,000, $20,000, $50,000,
but if you came into the office with $100,000, it was
almost impossible to get the policy.

*But you raised the sights of the industry when you
began writing the million-dollar policy. Now you're
selling even bigger ones. Those are the ones I want
to sell. Can I buy them?*

The underwriting committee often doesn't want to
give you a multi-million-dollar policy. They don't want
that much risk. They don't even want a share of that

much risk. Right now [this year] I have $50 million on the books paid and another $60 million I haven't yet been able to get. I have cases that have been examined, but every time the mail comes, there's another request: We don't want this, we want this; we want another X-ray; we want another inspection report. They're reluctant. If you want a $100,000 policy, there are a hundred agents and a thousand companies that will get it for you tomorrow. Add a couple more zeros to the amount, and they don't want it.

Why are the underwriters afraid to take the risk?

As with many companies, New York Life policies are incontestable after just two years. Let's suppose you're holding a great big bundle of life insurance that's incontestable. Even if you committed suicide, even if you took an overdose of medication, we'd have to pay off. So you might do drastic things, things you wouldn't normally do. You know, you pick up the paper and read, "The man hit a bridge in broad daylight." No one can understand what happened. But he's dead.

Does that mean the underwriters must look into a prospect's character and activities as well as his or her medical record?

Yes. Let's suppose they find out that you like other men's wives. They'll turn you down quicker on moral grounds than if they found out that you don't have a good, sound financial program.

Say you're on a program of corporate acquisition. You acquire the XYZ company. It's losing a lot of money, say, a million-dollar loss. Your company is doing nothing but making money. You put those two companies together. You use the loss to cover your income tax. You acquire that company with Uncle Sam paying the bill. If you spread this kind of activity too thin, the underwriting committee will turn you down.

Underwriters will turn you down not only for medical reasons but also just because they don't like what you're doing. They don't want large amounts of insurance unless there's a really good reason why the person needs it. I sometimes send an application into our home office and say I want a million. They'll come back and say, "What for?" I'll say, "He's in debt and owes a million!" They'll say, "Why should we pay it?"

As a rule, to be able to get your life insured, you better measure up financially and morally as well as physically. Lead a good life!

You see, the big policy is harder to buy than it is to sell. You're doing a real service for that man or woman if you can get it. Get everything put together, get him or her a thorough exam, then see what your life underwriting committee will tell you. New York Life now will not hesitate on a five-hundred-thousand–dollar case—but send down a multi-million–dollar case! I had a $5-million case recently. They not only didn't want it, they didn't want any part of it. They would rather have ten people, each insured for $250,000, than one person insured for $2.5 million.

So sometimes you have to sell life underwriting as well as the prospect.

I submit all my cases to New York Life. If they turn a case down, and it's a "must" case where I have to get insurance, then I'll look to other companies. Naturally, I try to favor my own company first, but if it doesn't work out, then I try somewhere else.

PART 3

Chapter 56

How to Find the Freedom to Sell

If I had your volume, Ben, I'd never be able to set foot out of the office. How do you do it? How can I get that really important freedom—the freedom to sell?

Get adequate office help and good equipment. Learn to delegate. Learn time control: Establish priorities. Make use of procedures. Use the spread sheet and daily cards. Make up tomorrow's appointments today.

What do you mean by "delegate"?

I feel that you should invest money in yourself. You're in business. Do you know of a businessowner who can operate a business without capital—without investing in himself? After a while you become a little more knowledgeable, and when you do—delegate. Don't do what your secretary can do. When you find that you need a second secretary, get one. Don't spend your time doing what someone can do for four or six or eight dollars an hour. Spend money! It will make you money! There's nothing quite for nothing.

Delegate to people and machines what they can do so you can do what you do best.

Why are "priorities" important?

I found out a long, long time ago that you've got to do first things first. You've got to have a system of priorities. If you don't, you'll get buried in detail.

Can you show me samples of your spread sheets and daily cards?

Here they are.

NOVEMBER 1, 1973

PLANNER-PAD

Your Success in Attaining Your Objective Is Primarily the Result of the Effective Use of Time — — "THOSE WHO PLAN AHEAD . . . GET AHEAD"

PROSPECTS	PROSPECTS (continued)	EXAMINED	ISSUED	BINDERS	BROKERAGE

Planner-Pad, developed and copyrighted by H. Preston Smith, C.L.U., Denver, Co.

NEW NAMES SECURED TODAY

NAME   ADDRESS AND DATE OF BIRTH

1

2

3

4

5

TO SEE TODAY

DATE _____

FORENOON

NAME   ADDRESS

1
2
3
4
5
6

AFTERNOON

1
2
3
4
5
6

EVENING

TELEPHONE

Chapter 57

The Successful Selling Routine

Tell us a little bit about your typical day.

My office is just a stone's throw from my home. I get in about 8:00 A.M. About an hour later, one of the secretaries brings in all the mail. Someone else has gone through the mail, and I get only what I should be looking at.

I'll ask my secretary to come in. She's the person who does the correspondence. I'll get an idea and I'll say, "Put this down, put this down, put this down." She'll make up rough memos. I'll write a number of letters. I don't have to dictate. I'll just say, 'Write a letter to so and so and tell him this." She knows my thinking well enough. You see, I'm delegating. I'm saving the time that I would have used if I had to dictate the letter myself. She and I will spend maybe half an hour together.

Then the head of my Program Department comes in. She brings in a long list of cases. She asks me which of these I must have. I'll say, "I've got to have this one. I've got to have that one." I'll tell her, "Make me up a Split Dollar on so and so." Or, "Make me up a tax illustration." Or, "Make me up this or that or something else." She has another person who helps her. I'll spend about 30 minutes with her.

I have a well-trained C.L.U. office administrator who does my service work. He can do most of it himself, but there are problem cases of all kinds. He'll run these by me.

By the way, it's this service man's job to make sure a prospect gets examined. He'll call the man or woman on the phone after I've left, and he'll say, "Mr. Feldman asked me to call you. I have an appointment set for Tuesday at 3:00 or Friday at 4:00." The prospect will say: "What for? I haven't bought any insurance!" My service man will say, "I don't know, he just asked me to call you!" It may sound crazy, but it works. Try it! It will work.

It's my administrator's job to follow through and get all the medical requirements fulfilled. The company may want a statement from Dr. Brown and Dr. Smith, or they may ask for an electrocardiograph or the Double Master's Test, etc. That's his job. I don't want to nag my prospect. I don't want to go near the prospect until I have something to sell. When the policies finally come in, I decide what it is I want to present and in what manner. It's up to me, and I go back to see him. Maybe he'll feel he's a busy man and I'm a busy man. Just a word on a piece of paper could mean so much. "Let's pin it down and then we'll have

30-60 days to work with your lawyer," I'll say. Three times out of four he'll go along—that's my ratio. I'll place three out of four cases.

I try to get out of the office before noon. I don't always, though, because there are always a million phone calls coming in. A lot of calls came in the day before. There's a little chalkboard in back of my desk with the messages. At 8:00 in the morning I have a lot of phone calls rolling out, but most of the people aren't in, and I leave word for them to call back. They do, and you know, that means another pair of hands!

It's a relief for me to get out of the office. I have a radio set-up built into my car as well as a cellular telephone. If something does take place, if someone calls in, if something happens that makes it necessary to reach me, they *can* reach me. They just call me. Doesn't matter where I am, they can reach me at once.

I go along, making calls on a list I've made up the night before. I carry a little card in my pocket with maybe eight or ten names on it—to place policies, to try to complete an exam, or to get an interview. I'll walk in, make notes. The recording machine in my car is an indispensable tool for note taking.

It goes on like this for the rest of the day. Much of my work is within a radius of about 40 miles from my home. About 7:00 or 7:30 P.M. I'll call my home and ask if anything took place that I should know about; if anyone called in or if there are any messages from the office. If there's anything I can do about the messages, I do it.

I bring a briefcase of work home with me. By now I'm so hungry—because I never take time for lunch and never take time for dinner until I get home—that when I walk into the kitchen, I have what I call a "take-back" sandwich. I make myself a great big sandwich and "take it back" into my bedroom. While I undress, I eat my sandwich. I get out of my clothes and put on comfortable clothes. After I eat dinner, I work for an hour or two getting ready for tomorrow—earmarking, perfecting the proposals I want made up the next day, maybe running over the dictation and picking out the things that are most important—things that really are the keys to the cases.

My day runs from 8:00 in the morning until 8:00 at night, with a couple of more hours thrown in to get ready for tomorrow. You see, there's no half–way. You either do it or you don't.

Now that doesn't mean I work all the time. When I get tired, I go fishing for two or three days. From my home in Florida, it's only a short distance into the Florida Keys, and I know a man down there who is part fish! He can really find them, whether they're biting or not. I get way out in a little boat—away from everything, not a sound to bother me. It's kind of good to be away. But after a couple of days, I feel better and I go back to work.

Chapter 58

How to Get Ideas That Pay Off

Ben, your success is based largely on your ideas. How can I get successful ideas of my own?

No one has a corner on ideas. You're successful because you have listened to other successful people. Get inspiration from others.

You can also learn from your own experiences. In sales work, the biggest mistake is not to make any mistakes.

Chapter 59

How to Build Self-Confidence

You've told me the way you sell successfully,
but there's one thing you haven't told me:
Just how can I feel confident enough to go out and
sell. What's your advice?

Accept yourself. Our ability to improve is dependent first of all upon accepting ourselves as we are now with our strong points and our weaknesses. Then always be engaged in some type of self-improvement.

Remember, progress is mental in origin. We know that thinking habits develop a self-hypnotic influence. The subconscious operates on the basis of images, not words. That's why we first must supply the mental equivalent of what we wish to achieve. Today and every day, act in accordance with the mental picture you have of yourself—your self-image.

Your confidence in yourself is determined by your personal estimate of your ability to handle the situation. Self-confidence is based upon past success. Think back to identical or similar situations that you handled successfully.

Also, *look* successful at all times.

Chapter 60

The "Magic Formula" for Success

If you had to sum up your formula for success in a few sentences, what would you say?

My formula for success?

I don't know, other than I really believe, and I try to be realistic: Nothing for nothing. Most people buy not because they believe but because the salesperson believes.

And something else that's very important. You know, I'm very happy to answer questions, but once in a while, there is somebody who wants a magic answer. "What's the 'magic formula' for success?" My magic formula has always been hard work.

Chapter 61

Feldmanisms and Power Phrases

Editor's Note: Many of the following Feldmanisms and Power Phrases are extracted from this book. We recommend that you read them, enjoy them, and then get started—if you haven't done so already—developing a working file of Power Phrases of your own, molded to your *own* inimitable style and delivery, just as Ben has done through the years. And bear in mind, as Ben points out, that "it's not *what* you say so much as *how* you say it." The sincerity in your voice, how you look at a prospect, is *really* what generates so much of the power in a Power Phrase.

I sell discounted dollars . . . may I show you?

We simply create the cash to pay what "must" be paid rather than risk loans and liquidations.

Let's use insurance to . . . keep together what you put together.

Do you have anyone on your payroll earning $1,000 per day? . . . you are!

We are on the risk for one million dollars and would like to reevaluate your life expectancy. Wouldn't you like to know?

Do you think the bank will extend the same credit line to the person who takes your place?

You know, you are the biggest asset on the balance sheet. Why shouldn't you be insured for what you are worth?

Wouldn't corporate credit be improved if your keypeople were insured?

Did you ever compare the return on money with the return on a keyperson?

How much is your life worth? How much did you insure it for?

May I talk to you about the $500,000 I owe you?

Let's insure your standard of living for your family.

We sell contracts for time and money. We can't guarantee the time, but we can guarantee the money.

Expand your partner's insurance because the day he "walks out" his wife may want her "money out."

We have a special policy designed to discount your tax. May I show it to you?

It's not feasible to carry in cash the amount of cash your estate will need. Better to do it with a tax policy.

Every person in a growing company has some unfinished business . . . such as a note at the bank.

When a person dies, a lot of problems come walking in the door.

Remember, as time goes by, people grow—and as they grow, quite often their problems grow. The need is greater. So the solution must be greater.

If you can't put aside 3 percent of the amount now . . . where would 100 percent come from later? Buy a little less . . . but begin now.

Make up two checks . . . one for the premium and one for the proceeds. Then just say . . . "you sign the little one . . . I'll sign the big one."

Mr. Jones, you have a problem. No one has a lease on life and most men never die at the right time; there is no right time, Mr. Jones, the taxes must be paid from your estate—or for your estate. Let me pay it for your estate—with discounted dollars.

There's a price tag on everything. By doing nothing, it will cost you dollars. By doing something, it will cost you pennies.

A positive mental attitude, that more than anything else determines your success. If you decide you are going to feel wonderful, strong, excited—then you have the power to move mountains.

O.K., I'll come back in five years. But if you're not here, whom shall I ask for?

The best prospect is the person with a problem—all kinds of assets, but no money.

As a rule, you will sell each year ten times the amount of insurance you own. Build your own program up to one million dollars, and you'll be writing ten million dollars a year.

Let me make sure you're as good on the inside as you look on the outside. Could be you've waited too long. As the years go by, a person pays a price for success. Mother nature makes us a little bit older. And older doesn't mean better. Let's see if you can qualify.

The start of a sale is in the interview. But the start of the interview is getting a prospect's attention. Unless you get his or her attention, you'll go no place.

In the interview, logic isn't enough. Use logic and emotion. Get the prospect stirred up. There's nothing like a disturbing question to build a fire under a person.

Never back a prospect into a corner and make him or her make a decision. Don't push. Lead.

Yes, you're in wonderful shape now. But your doctor didn't tell you how you'll be ten years from now. You see, we're going to take a look at how long you might live. Don't you want to know?

Most people buy not because they believe but because the salesperson believes.

You've got a good many people working for you. Why don't you hire one more? Me. Put me on your payroll. One hundred dollars a day. Set up a special account for me, and put $100 a day in it, and I'll set up a special account for you and put $1,000,000 in it! You know, it's going to take a long, long time for you to put in what you're someday going to take out. Suppose I put it together and you take a look?

Never underestimate your prospect's needs. When you underestimate his needs, you're not helping him. When you think small, you're actually hurting the person you should be helping.

How would you like to be a millionaire? Put me on your payroll for $100 a day—and the day you walk out, one million dollars walks in. Plus about 75 percent of the amount you paid in. Let me put it together. . . .

You know, there are two kinds of mistakes: Little ones and big ones. The little ones, the company can absorb. The big ones? They'll absorb the company.

The mistake a lot of us make, you see, is to look for extra money. If you reach down in a man's pocket for his wallet, he'll break your arm.

When you save money in a bank, that's an accumulation. But we create money for you. Who else can do that?

Doing nothing doesn't solve your problem; it only postpones it. You have a right to postpone it. But if you postpone solving your problem, you know who'll have to solve it? Your spouse.

If you have trouble paying pennies on the dollar, do you think your family will have it easy paying what must be paid with full hundred-cent dollars?

Why do you want to run hard for 30 years and then have 15 years go down the drain? You know, there's a price if you do something or if you don't do something. Most estates, someday, fall apart—not because you did something wrong but because you did nothing; that's what's wrong.

Epilogue

Ben, a lot of years have gone by since 1939 when you left your $10 a week butter-and-egg route and started your life insurance career. Now we're on the threshold of a new century. What advice would you give a person considering a career in life insurance today?

The decision I made at age 26 was a good one for me. And not just in terms of income. For the right young person with the right philosophy and the right outlook, I would highly recommend a career in life insurance. There are no limits, no ceiling on earnings. And there's a tremendous amount of satisfaction because you have an unlimited opportunity to serve others. With a piece of paper, a drop of ink, and a few pennies we can create security. Something most people want but do not have. Our product is designed to make the individual independent—free from reliance on government and welfare.

Also, the product itself is better than ever. The life insurance policy was *always* a fabulous instrument.

Yet life insurance is a much better buy today than it was way back when. You can buy a contract for $20,000 a year, and in less than ten years it's paid off, and you've got a million dollars set aside for your family the day you walk out.

Ben, what effect has the personal computer had on your office procedure and sales efforts?

The personal computer has become a valuable "member" of our office staff. I doubt whether there's any other industry in which the ease and availability of personal computers has had a greater effect. Concepts that were cost-prohibitive before—illustrations that would have taken two, three, four hours to calculate by hand—can now be run in minutes.

Our illustration hardware is a basic IBM PC XT, which has been upgraded several times. We do our best to keep up with the new trends. If I am told we need new software, we get it. If our hardware no longer has the capabilities, we upgrade. You either roll with the new computer technology or get rolled over by it. If you don't keep abreast of the latest software, you can be sure your competition will, and you'll be left in the dust.

But the computer won't prospect for you, although it can be of great help in organizing your prospecting procedure. And it won't replace the power you get from knowing your product, your prospect's problem, and how life insurance can solve it.

Ben, as I understand it, you're still strictly "plain vanilla" life insurance. You don't do financial planning in terms of dealing with equity products. Can you comment on your feelings about financial planning?

No, I'm not in financial planning, although my sons Richard and Marvin are. For me, the basis of a person's security is still life insurance. You know, financial planning to me is managing money. And you can't *manage* money until you *have* money. Most people don't have enough money. Trying to accumulate enough capital so that you can have money at work, money at risk, can take a long, long time. And we underwrite that time. Time is the greatest asset you can have. It enables you both to create and conserve.

Financial planners try to determine how much tolerance for risk their clients have. And rightly so. With life insurance, we transfer that risk to an insurance company. Life insurance doesn't really insure a life. It insures a promise ... a vision ... an intention. It insures money ... savings ... assets ... wealth. Life insurance is the heart of financial planning.

Does that mean that you would advise the young career-seeker to stick with life insurance and not get involved with financial planning?

No, of course not. What is right for me may not be right for the next person. It all boils down to this: You don't *have* to be a financial planner or a business insurance expert or a pension specialist to do well. But whatever you decide to be, you have to know your business. Knowledge is power. The more knowledge you have, the more effective you can be!

Find what people want. Find their problems and the price tags on their problems. Then demonstrate a very simple solution. So simple that it becomes foolish not to do it.

Dream a little—visualize where you want to be. Now you build a road, step by step. Continue going uphill. It makes you bigger and better. You know you can. Take that first step. Begin. Oh sure, you will stub your toe now and then, but you know why? You're climbing—going uphill. Never stop.

Index

About the Author

Ben Feldman is generally acknowledged to be the world's greatest life insurance salesman and one of the nation's all-time great salesmen in any field.[1] After giving up a $10 a week job as an egg peddler for his father, he began his career in life insurance as a debit salesman in 1938. Three years later he joined New York Life and, at the urging of his manager, concentrated on selling business insurance. That was the beginning of his meteoric rise to the zenith of success in both earnings and accomplishments, beyond doubt the most remarkable career in the history of life insurance selling.

He was the recipient of the 1984 John Newton Russell Memorial Award, the highest honor in the life insurance industry.

Ben Feldman has written individual life insurance coverages totaling more than $1 billion. He has an annual average of about $22 million in coverage over 45 years and in a single year has sold as much as $100 million.

Feldman's sales methods were the subject of a best-selling book by his former manager, Andy Thomson.[2] *Creative Selling*, by Ben Feldman, represents a reinforcement and extension of his sales methods. Its format—answers to questions about his philosophy and selling methods—is a natural one for Ben since the questions are selected from those he's asked most frequently in platform appearances throughout the nation and abroad.

---

[1] B.C. Forbes, *America's Twelve Master Salesmen* (B.C. Forbes, 1952); Edwin P. Hoyt, *The Supersalesmen* (World Publishing Co., 1962); Perrin Stryker, *The Incomparable Salesmen* (McGraw Hill, 1967).

[2] Andrew H. Thomson. *The Feldman Method* (Longman Financial Services Publishing, Inc., 1989).